T0355704

The Morning Myth

How Every Night Owl Can Become More Productive, Successful, Happier, and Healthier

Frank J. Rumbauskas

WILEY

To my two beautiful daughters, Agnes and Maeve. I cannot possibly imagine my life without you both in it. You have made me a better person and brought me happiness beyond my wildest dreams. I love nothing more than simply being with you, and your Dad will always be there for you. No matter what.

Contents

Preface

If you're a "night owl," I feel your pain. I'm one, too. I know what it's like to be judged by others as being lazy, slothful, and juvenile, when in fact studies continually show that night owls achieve more in life and the majority are wealthier and more consistently successful than morning people.

You may find that hard to believe after years of being brainwashed with the notion that morning people are more successful, and somehow just plain *better*, than we are, but it's true. I'm living proof of it.

And the endless criticism we suffer can be unbearable at times.

Friends who I call my "office neighbors" sometimes comment on how late I arrive to the office. What they don't know is how extremely productive and creative I am after the sun sets in the evening.

About 10 years ago, I had a television interview scheduled for 8:00 a.m. at my office. When the TV crew arrived, my receptionist told them, "Frank is never here this early!" The look on her face as I came through the door was priceless!

Even family and friends get in on the act, when they should be the very people who support us. They simply assume that because I've been fortunate to experience tremendous success in my businesses that I'm "fat and happy" and sleep in for the sheer hell of it. Nothing could be further from the truth; the reality is that I sleep in later than most because *that is what makes me hyperproductive.*

They're all wrong, as you'll learn in a minute, and I have good news for you: If you're a night owl, there's nothing wrong with you!

Take it from Kate Shellnut at Vox.com:

Night owls aren't the lazy, distracted weirdos the early crowd makes us out to be. When the rest of the world winds down, we work, create, and tinker on our own schedules. Each evening, I watch the typical bedtimes pass by and wait for that jolt of energy and inspiration that comes well past twilight...

For us, staying up late is the easy part. The real challenge comes when we wake up and face the early risers, who still see night owls as lazy, juvenile, and unhealthy. And today's hyperawareness around the importance of sleep has only made our reputations worse...

Night owls remain a misunderstood, maligned minority. We defy the conventional wisdom, missing out on the proverbial worm and whatever instincts make early risers "healthy, wealthy, and wise."

Both family and friends, aside from my wife and kids, are completely unaware that during my waking hours, I work almost constantly, and produce my very best work after the sun has set and the kids and my wife are in bed; she just happens to be a morning person, and thankfully, one who understands that I perform best on a night owl schedule.

Early to bed, early to rise, makes a man healthy, wealthy, and wise.

—**Ben Franklin**˙

You just learned that Ben Franklin's famous quote has it all wrong when it comes to being wealthier.

The news gets worse for morning people—they're not healthier, either. They're not necessarily less healthy; however, Franklin's quote has once again been proven wrong, and to make matters worse, night owls who force themselves to get up early may in fact suffer from diminished cognitive function and decreased immunity, and are at higher risk for depression, anxiety, and seasonal affective disorder. That's why it's insane for nearly all employers to require that employees arrive at 8:00 a.m. First of all, night owls who are forced to work on that schedule may not perform as well, and second, they'll probably have more sick days, which means lost productivity to the employer. (Maybe that's why antidepressants and anti-anxiety medications are the most prescribed drugs in the United States and many other Western nations?)

Considering the fact that approximately 32% of people are night owls—almost one-third of the population, with many estimates going up to half—forcing 100% of employees to be at work early is simply foolish, and the worst part is that a large percentage of employers, who are successful night owls, make their staff come in at 8:00 a.m. while they're at home sleeping until 9:00 a.m. or later. It's costing employers more money than

˙I learned from reading Mark Twain's books that his grandfather was close friends with Benjamin Franklin, and that Franklin was part of the "do as I say, not as I do" crowd. In fact, he admitted himself that he awakened at 9:00 a.m. every day and stayed in bed to read the morning newspaper. The lesson: Don't believe everything you hear unless it's supported by evidence!

those employees are generating. If they would schedule work-days around employees' sleep tendencies, they'd have infinitely more productive "night owl" employees if they let them come in from 11:00 a.m. to 5:00 p.m., and allowed them to work from home after dark, when they're at their very best.

Don't Try to Change Your Sleep Habits

I'm also going to venture a guess that you have tried to be a so-called "morning person" and found the results to be disastrous. I've been there, too.

(The brainwashing that causes us to attempt to become early risers is explained in later in the book.)

You see, I was born with low thyroid function, which was not discovered until about three years ago, after my wife and I signed on with a private concierge doctor. We made that decision after Obamacare wrecked our health insurance and we found ourselves paying $2,000/month for insurance that covered virtually nothing. The concierge practice we joined conducts an extremely thorough three-hour exam and extensive lab work when on-boarding a new patient, including a take-home adrenal saliva test kit.

Finding the correct dose of thyroid hormone is very difficult. Taking replacement thyroid hormone throws lab tests way off, so the only accurate way to determine the proper dosage is to monitor symptoms, energy levels, and midday body temperature.

At one point in this grand experiment, I was taking too much and began suffering from hyperthyroidism.

As if by magic, I began waking between 5:45 a.m. and 6:00 a.m.

The problem is, my work output, income, and overall wealth dropped instead of increasing. I was astonished because I was excited to finally be an early riser and be hyperproductive, but it didn't work out that way.

To make matters worse, I began to get sick and catch colds more often. Research proves that attempting to fight your natural sleep cycle is harmful to your health, and reduces immunity in particular. If the drop in productivity weren't bad enough already, now I was having downtime due to repeated illness, particularly nasty colds that always seemed to be followed by sinus infections.

My night owl brain wasn't working at full power on that schedule, despite the fact that I was bursting with energy. Needless to say, my doctor and I agreed to drop the dosage and I fell back into my normal circadian rhythm. (By the way, and contrary to popular belief, you cannot change your circadian rhythm, which will be explained later in the book as well.)

Other attempts to force myself to go to sleep early with the help of a sleep aid, and wake up early, were also disasters. I was downright miserable and tired all day, and the bags under my eyes didn't help much in meetings with prospective clients, or even in performing simple tasks such as answering email. My body simply wanted to get up later. It needed to sleep in its own schedule, not one invented by society. (By the way, this whole "start work at eight o'clock" nonsense goes back to agrarian farming days—in other words, the world is still operating on a schedule that's ancient history nowadays.)

But don't take it from me. Here are just a few examples of scientific research done on the topic:

- A study done at the Institute of Neuroscience and Medicine in Germany found that when night owls follow the same time schedules as morning people, there's a tendency to develop seasonal affective disorder or depression. Researchers at the University of Liege in Belgium conducted a study in which night owls and morning people competed against each other to measure reaction and attention times. When given a task shortly after waking up, both groups did well, but 10 hours after their days began, the night owls were better at completing assigned tasks and were quicker and more alert. Dr. Victoria Sharma, medical director of the Sharp Grossmont Hospital's Sleep Disorders Center, said morning larks can be perceived as more driven at work because they tend to perform better early in the day, while a night owl's circadian rhythm may be telling them they should still be sleeping. (*Fast Company*)

• Sharma carried out a study among 59 people and found that night owls and morning larks have different brain structures that cannot be changed. (*Huffington Post*)

• Researchers at Southampton University in England analyzed a national sample of men and women who'd been surveyed years earlier on sleep patterns as well as measures related to, well, health, wealth, and wisdom. There were 356 morning larks in the group (in bed before 11 p.m., up before 8 a.m.) and 318 night owls (in bed after 11 p.m., up after 8 a.m.). Contrary to Ben Franklin's decree, night owls had larger incomes and more access to cars than did morning larks; the two chronotypes also scored roughly the same on a cognitive test and showed no self- or doctor-reported health differences. "We found no evidence … that following Franklin's advice about going to bed and getting up early was associated with any health, socioeconomic, or cognitive advantage," the authors concluded. "If anything, owls were wealthier than larks, though there was no difference in their health or wisdom." (*Fast Company*)

• The results showed that evening types scored higher than morning types on inductive reasoning, which has been shown to be a good estimate of general intelligence and one of the strongest predictors of academic performance. A further piece of good news for the owls is that inductive reasoning is linked to innovative thinking and more prestigious occupations, and tends to lead to higher incomes. Famous night owls include former president Barack Obama, Charles Darwin, Winston Churchill, James Joyce, Marcel Proust, Keith Richards, and Elvis Presley, to name a few. (*The Independent*)

- Night people are more intelligent: Psychologist Richard D. Roberts of the University of Sydney and Patrick C. Kyllonen of the Air Force Research Lab completed a study into chronotypes in 1999 published in *Personality and Individual Differences*. They measured the chronotypes of 420 test participants, then administered intelligence tests. The study found that night people marginally outperformed morning people on most of the intelligence measures. The most significant differences were found in working memory and processing speed. These findings were true even when the tests were taken in the morning. (*Learning Mind*)

- Morning people aren't wealthier: Catharine Gale and Christopher Martyn from MRC Environmental Epidemiology Unit, Southampton University, also studied chronotypes. They analyzed a national sample of men and women who'd been surveyed years earlier on sleep patterns as well as measures related to health, wealth, and wisdom. The group included 356 morning larks and 318 night owls. The results showed that overall night owls had larger incomes than larks. (*Learning Mind*)

Why I Did All This Research

The obvious reason I researched and wrote this book was to eliminate the belief that there's something wrong with me (or you) or that we're "lazy" for being late risers. No, it wasn't to make myself feel better about being a night owl, although that did happen!

I did it to refute a free report written and distributed by a friend and fellow best-selling author as a "lead magnet" to get people into his website and buy his time-management program. The report claimed that the one thing all billionaires and other highly successful people have in common is that they're very early risers, as in rising at 4:00 to 5:00 a.m.

I called *BS!*

Why? Because there is no proof to back that up.

I chose to do my own research, with the help of a research assistant, and what I found astonished me: Night owls overall are more successful than morning people! At a minimum I assumed we all performed the same, overall, but merely at different times. The reality, however, is that night owls are more prosperous in general.

Comparing the traits and habits that these people had in common not only refuted the report's claim, but in general revealed nothing other than the fact that morning people have a circadian rhythm at or close to 24 hours, while night owls were on the other end of that scale, with a circadian rhythm of somewhere between 24.5 and 25 hours. It's that extra hour our body wants that makes us get up later than others, and makes us feel exhausted all day when we don't get it.

This is genetic, it's permanent, and it cannot be changed!

How to Use This Book

The purpose of this book is fourfold:

1. To cure you of any insecurity or belief that there's something wrong with you, or that you're "lazy" for rising later than morning people—and to restore your self-confidence. Have you ever noticed how morning people can't state

that they are early birds without sounding as if they are asking "Aren't I a goody-goody?" I've noticed it, too, and it's arrogant and unnecessary. Sadly, these are the same people behind the popular myth that night owls are "lazy." Heck, maybe we should start calling them out on their inability to keep up with us past mid- to late afternoon! After all, studies show that the early bird may catch the worm, but he can't go the distance. Morning people typically begin to fade and lose a significant degree of concentration, cognitive function, and memory shortly after 3:00 p.m. every day. Night owls, on the other hand, can go the distance, and are productive for far more hours each day than morning people.

2. To show you how to make the most of your night owl circadian rhythm, and how to make it work for you and not against you—and outperform all those goody-goody morning people! I'm also going to tell you what to avoid in your diet that may interfere with sleep and help you to be more productive than you ever previously imagined.

3. To help you enjoy better health. After all, scientists have learned that waking before daylight is harmful for your health and throwing off natural sleep patterns can cause hormonal imbalances and increase risks of heart disease, stroke, diabetes, and depression! That's because when daylight comes, your body stops producing melatonin, the sleep hormone, and a spike in cortisol occurs to help you to wake up. But if you rise before dawn, your body is still producing melatonin unless you use a sleep therapy light when you awaken, which still takes considerable time to work. The cortisol rush doesn't come until daylight, and if you rose before dawn, it will present as anxiety or "the jitters," which in turn raises blood pressure and overall wreaks havoc on those two all-important hormones, among many

others. High cortisol also massively decreases immune function, so if you get to work bright and early and the person in the next cubicle is sneezing and coughing, don't be surprised if you get sick too.

4. To teach employers how to get the most productivity possible from employees by working with them on schedules based upon their natural sleep cycles.

So if you've been self-conscious about your night owl-ness, or suffer from low self-confidence, and are tired of the criticism that far too many morning people throw at us, rest assured. You now know that you're at a distinct advantage over them, and now you're going to learn how to use your night owl tendencies to get ahead, be successful, and, as Ben Franklin put it, to be a healthy, wealthy, and wise night owl!

I wish you all the best and am glad that you're also a part of the night owl family!

Frank J. Rumbauskas
October 2018
Dallas, Texas

1

Confessions of a Stigmatized Night Owl

How Early Rising Nearly Destroyed My Business (and Did Destroy My Education)

Let me tell you my own personal story of the living hell of being a night owl in a society that seems to begin the workday at the crack of dawn, while I would have preferred getting up at the crack of noon all the while.

A Very Annoyed Five-Year-Old

No matter how far back I think in my lifetime, I can always remember being forced out of bed earlier than I should have been.

The memories go all the way back to elementary school. Maybe it was kindergarten, maybe it was first grade. All I remember is my mom coming into my bedroom, turning on the lights, setting out clothes for me to wear for the day, and haranguing me to get moving.

She didn't mean anything negative by it. (I love you, Mom!) She only wanted me to do well in school, having been raised in a generation when school actually mattered. After all, school is school and we couldn't control what time the school day started.

Even now, despite our kids naturally waking around 7:00 a.m. on most days, we sometimes have to gently wake them, particularly our youngest who tends to take after me rather than my wife. Oh, and if anyone doesn't like being woken too early, it's my younger daughter, Maeve! (Well, besides myself, that is, although, ironically, she does go to bed on her own when she's tired. If we're visiting family or vice versa, she'll even fight to go to bed! Thankfully she's easily guilt-tripped. "But everyone is here just to see *you!*" She eats that one up.)

I remember those boring school days as if I were still there. The experience of spending all day in school watching the clock, trying to pay attention, watching the clock, sitting in a hard wooden desk that I can still smell, watching the clock, sweating my ass off both early and late in the school year (public schools in Linden, New Jersey, didn't have air conditioning back then), and dreading the day's homework assignments. Did I mention watching the clock? In fact, it was the boredom and rigidity of traditional schooling that compelled my wife and me to send our kids to private school—or at least to the type of school where learning is made to be fun and kids learn by doing, not by drudg-ery and rote memorization. (The school's motto is that a child is a lamp to be lighted, not a vessel to be filled with useless infor-mation. I couldn't agree more, though they don't actually use the words "useless information." I added that.)

Perhaps more accurately, school was boring and rigid for *me*. That's most likely because I would have rather slept in for a couple of extra hours and actually been *ready* for the day, but I neither had a choice in the matter, nor did I have any idea I was a night owl. However, not all kids are natural night owls to begin with, and not all teenagers tend to be extreme night owls. (If you're in doubt, and you have teenage kids, think of the fun of getting them to bed on time! Although if their grades suck, now you know why. Hopefully.) Other kids enjoyed school. Some even loved it. I didn't. Don't get me wrong; my grades were stel-lar and I almost always brought home straight A's, at least before I checked my brain out of school entirely. I just hated being dragged out of bed to sit in a classroom to learn boring subjects that I'd never use in real life, especially when they were taught primarily by people who never left school in the first place!

Like any good kid, I told my parents I liked school. After all, I had good grades and didn't want to disappoint them. But I hated it. And I never fully understood why.

At least not until about 10 years later.

High School Hell

High school was hell. No, not the kind of high school that you see in 1980s movies, with the jocks throwing the nerds in lockers and giving them wedgies and all that, though that certainly went on. (And high school for me really was in the 1980s.) Granted, I was a nerd, but got along well with most anyone, just like I still do today. The only difference is that I was a major introvert as a kid and I'm an extrovert as an adult, the result of a very successful sales career followed by lots and lots of public speaking as a best-selling author. Or at least I think that's why. I met my wife in 2004 and she still refuses to believe that I was ever an introvert, while my family back in New Jersey cannot fathom the concept that I'm now extroverted and love to show up at networking mixers and business roundtables and the Rotary Club (which is full of younger people now—it's not your grandpa's Rotary Club anymore), Dad's nights put on by both the school and by us on our own time, and other venues where I could meet and mingle with new people.

After all, what I primarily do for a living—high-level sales process consulting with VPs and C-Suite executives—isn't exactly conducive to networking. CEOs don't go to networking mixers, nor do VPs; they're simply too busy. Nor would they benefit from them, either. Indeed, they'd find themselves surrounded by people who cannot help them, and you don't reach the C-Suite by wasting time. So when I go to an event, it's to enjoy good conversation and the company of others.

Compare that to when I was 10 years old or so and would go hide in my room when relatives came to visit. I'm being totally serious.

(If you're wondering how I can talk and work with CEOs on their level without an education, the *Harvard Business Review* "Essentials" series is beyond valuable. You'll learn everything you need to know and save a hundred grand on that MBA!)

It was in middle school that I stopped bringing home straight A grades. Okay, I wasn't bringing home D's and F's either, but in my house, all hell broke loose without all A's on the report card. (Thank God my kids don't have to deal with report cards, for their sakes!)

Natural Law stated that, as a nerd, I must hate gym class, which I did. In middle school I used to just cut gym and instead do some extra credit work in a science class, which always helped me to avoid getting busted for skipping gym. Besides, the locker room smelled something awful.

So when high school came around, I enrolled in the school's Navy JROTC (Junior Reserve Officer Training Corps). I had zero interest in the military, which would later change, thanks to JROTC, even though I never served. The reason I joined is because it replaced gym class. In other words, for four years of high school, I never had to attend gym class once. And that was okay because the physical training in JROTC was far superior to playing sports in gym class anyway! (Although that became a lot more fun as a senior when I was able to order the freshmen to do push-ups.)

There was a problem, though...

You see, for my first two years of high school, homeroom started at 8:05 a.m. After homeroom, instead of heading to gym class, I went across the street to Navy JROTC class every day.

It worked out great until I reached my junior year. Because both were able to hold officer ranks in our company, juniors and seniors were combined into one JROTC class, which was held at... [drum roll please]...7:15 a.m.!

Don't get me wrong—I loved JROTC. Loved it. I loved everything I learned, I loved hearing our instructors' war stories (literally), I loved putting on a Navy uniform once a week, I loved learning how to shoot well on rifle team...I just didn't love the early hour. About the only thing worse was being awakened by flying trashcans at 5:00 a.m. when they sent us to boot camp at the U.S. Coast Guard's recruit training facility in Cape May, New Jersey, known as "Camp Snoopy" to the drill instructors.

Can you seriously imagine me getting up so freaking early so I could get to school by 7:15 a.m.? Keep in mind that I frequently walked the mile from home to class. (Okay, fine, 0.9 miles.) Double the annoyance for having to salute some higher-ranking kids I didn't like, or the many times I slipped and fell on ice walking in the winter.

At least I was a step ahead of my best friend Tom from back in those days, who would often show up as late as 7:45 a.m., thanks to one shared bathroom in his house.

Just like now, if I have to get up super early, I do fine for a while, at least until the crash hits in the early to mid afternoon. (This happens to so-called morning people, too, though they'll deny it all the way to the grave. You'll learn the scientific and medical reasons why further on in this book.)

Having said all that, I actually looked forward to the class every day. In fact, for a nerd who initially had no interest in anything military, I came to love JROTC and it was not only my favorite class in high school, but the discipline learned there became a valuable lifetime skill and it still benefits me even today, nearly three decades after graduating from high school. My instructors have passed on and I only wish I could tell them how much they contributed to my success.

Obviously, the class wasn't the problem. The problem was later on. I did fine until lunchtime. Then I ate and the slump hit … but for me, the quintessential night owl, *it never went away*.

That's when my grades began to go to hell. (Which is why I didn't get into any of the military academies I applied to, nor did I get a college ROTC scholarship.) Indeed, it wasn't until I began outlining this book that I put two and two together and realized that my grades crashed *exactly* when I had to start getting up an hour earlier!

After dragging my way through the school day, struggling to understand subjects like mathematics and chemistry that I'd always aced without even trying, I came home each and every day and went straight to my bedroom for a nap.

Seriously, without exception, I needed to nap every single day after school once the start time changed to 7:15 a.m. Even today if I have to get up early—for example, I belonged to a weekly 7:30 a.m. business roundtable group until it disbanded— I still have to get that nap in sometime during the afternoon. If I don't, I get a much, much stronger "second wind" later on and then I cannot go to bed. (The "second wind" is another cortisol rush and, once it hits, good luck falling asleep.)

From High School to College Dropout

I never really wanted to go to college, but like I said, my parents grew up in the days when a degree wasn't yet a commodity and having one was worth a fortune. I bought into the same myth because I didn't know any better. I did beg and plead to take a year off before starting college, but that wasn't going to happen.

Off I went to college. After several years of being an amateur radio operator, something I started when I was 13 years old and continued through adulthood, particularly the public service aspect of it, I just *knew* I wanted to be an electrical engineer. I loved tinkering with electronics, and even had my first profitable business underway at 14 years old, buying antique radios for next to nothing at local swap meets (rarely more than five dollars), refurbishing them, then selling them via classified ads for over a hundred dollars each. That's big money for a teenager. On top of that I used to go to work with my dad at AT&T Technologies pretty frequently during the summer, and was fascinated by everything I saw there; I even got to witness the very first prototype of a surface-mount circuit board being robot-assembled. (I have a feeling that only my fellow nerds will know what that is without looking it up, although I know they're all drooling right now.)

My very first class as a college student blindsided me. It seemed too good to be true. (And it was.) We all showed up in the lecture hall at 8:00 a.m., the professor came in, announced that it was way too early in the morning to have a class, and moved it to a later hour. Wow! "This place was made for me," I thought. Wrong! All that meant was having 8:00 a.m. classes only four days a week instead of five. To add insult to injury, that professor turned out to be downright sadistic.

The big problem was that my final two years of high school—when I had to be there at 7:15 a.m. and was brain-fried by early afternoon—left me ill prepared for one of the world's toughest engineering schools.

That night owl professor happened to be my calculus professor. The problem was that I flunked calculus in high school; it was in the postcrash hours of the afternoon, and then I flunked it again in college. The extreme fatigue I experienced from having to get up too early, in both venues, essentially took my brain offline as soon as it set in. And I, for one, cannot remember a damned thing when I'm that tired.

After a lousy first semester, I went to intersession over Christmas break, which is a glorified two-week version of summer school that everyone passes, regardless of actual performance. It was around then that I realized that many private universities are for-profit businesses, not wonderful institutions of higher education. I later learned the reason everyone passed intersession was so that the school could keep the tuition dollars rolling in.

My second semester was a complete disaster. Friends would even come to my dorm room to try to wake me up for class. They knew that I was intelligent and could make it; however, they didn't understand the concept that I simply don't function well early in the morning.

To make matters worse, this was all during the recession of 1991–1992. I had pledged a fraternity, only to find 30-something-year-old men—with electrical engineering degrees—

living in the frat house due to unemployment. That was my first clue that maybe school wasn't worth it. My suspicions were confirmed when one of those electrical engineers couldn't wire a lamp plug and I had to do it for him! I thought I'd walk out of there after four years able to build radios and other electronics, and this joker couldn't do something that electricians learn on day one. This is why I continued to suspect that college is a scam.

It wasn't long before I fell so far behind from all those missed classes that there was no hope of catching up, so I spent the rest of the year partying and having fun. (Maybe that's when my introversion started to fade?) It all culminated in getting kicked out of the dorms for shooting off fireworks on campus and having to live "at home," as they say. (I guess I never understood that saying, since living with your parents means living with *your parents*, not living at *your* home.)

Then came the big decision: Go deeper into debt by spending another year in a school I hated, and, to add insult to injury, have to wake up at an insane hour in order to commute there?

No thanks. It was time to call it quits.

The College Dropout Enters the Workforce

With all the pro-college brainwashing I endured from parents, teachers, principals, and guidance counselors—you name it— only my burning desire to someday become wealthy overcame the inferiority complex I gained from being a high school graduate in a college-educated world.

Assuming I had no marketable skills other than my love of working on cars, I got a job as an auto mechanic. Some days were good; others were bad. It all depended on what kind of work came in each day. Having said that, going home every day all greasy and with transmission fluid in my hair flat-out sucked.

The bigger issue, however, was getting to work. Just like with everything else, the day started at 8:00 a.m. (Seriously, what is it about 8:00 a.m. that they are all addicted to?) For several months I was there on time, and then I began to fade. The early days started catching up with me and before long I was sleeping in every few weeks and not getting to work.

Finally, I decided enough was enough and I quit. I got a lecture from the owner on how I needed to go to mechanic school to learn "the computer," which was about the stupidest thing I'd ever heard, since using "the computer" is a matter of plugging in a cable, seeing what code comes up, looking it up in a book, then replacing the faulty part. Nowadays, that's all mechanics really do. I remember one time when the Land Rover dealership had my wife's car for a total of four weeks in separate visits. The thing is, I instantly knew what was wrong with it, but since there were no codes, the dealer's mechanics couldn't figure it out. Finally I got them on the phone, explained that when a car is stalling randomly and there are no codes being generated, it's an early fuel pump problem. (They called back two hours later to confirm that it was the fuel pump regulator. But I digress. Now I'm just bragging.)

Next up was my first sales job. Okay, not really my first, considering my amateur radio fixer-upper business, and a part-time telemarketing job I did at night during high school for a while.

This was a real job—the kind where you had to wear a tie, at a minimum. So tie shopping we all went. It was still telemarketing, but it was business-to-business, and I was very good at it. Great, in fact. Until I got tired of showing up by 8:00 a.m. to an office that was a solid 40-minute commute away on a good day.

I won't go into the details, because you already know enough to guess how it turned out.

Success Found—At Last!

Over the next few years I moved around a bit and held a variety of jobs, some in sales, others not.

Finally, I landed in Las Vegas, Nevada, which was the biggest growth city at the time; that's why I'd moved there. Common sense told me that where there is massive growth, there is massive opportunity in B2B sales, so I jumped all over it.

And that's when it happened.

Soon I found myself employed not just in sales, but in *outside sales*. For the first time ever, I could excel at a job—even be #1 in the office—and not have to be at work at 8:00 a.m.!

There was some culture shock involved, though. My wife, also from the New York City metro area, but whom I met in Phoenix, Arizona, had a similar experience upon moving to Phoenix.

The thing is, these cowboys and cowgirls from the Old West would brag about being up at 5:30 a.m.! Or 5:00 a.m.! Or 4:30 a.m.! It was like a big pissing contest to see who got up the earliest.

I can't remember how many times I'd set up an appointment with a prospect only to hear the words, and of course they said this braggingly, "I'm up every day at 5:00 a.m. How about you come by at 6:30?"

"How about 10:00? That's when I'm open. My morning is already booked." Yeah, with sleep, that is! They always bought it though and I got my deals done at times that worked for me.

Soon I was kicking ass and taking names in the sales game. Sure, I struggled for a long time while I took the idiotic advice to make cold calls all day, every day, but eventually I was hired by a sales manager with a brain who showed me the path to lightness and away from that ineffective, dark-side stuff known as cold calling.

The real reason I became a star at selling wasn't entirely because I learned how to get sales without the misery of cold calling, though that was huge. The primary reason was because I could largely set my own work schedule—no more mandatory 8:00 a.m. nonsense!

Before long I was in high demand and could name my price to competitors, though I stayed at that job until I relocated again to Phoenix in 2000. I was earning five figures a month and had a fantastic sales manager who was not only remote, but when he came to our office for a week each month, he left me alone. At most I'd get a voicemail on Thursday saying, "Hey Frank, it's John, just seeing how things are going and if you need to get together for any reason before I head back tomorrow." Of course he left those messages in the morning; I didn't get the message until I woke up.

Freedom Found

With the relative freedom my success in sales had brought me, I was finally happy.

And it was all because I didn't have to drag myself out of bed at an ungodly hour and then spend the rest of the day dragging ass and wondering what was wrong with me. It turns out there's nothing wrong with me; the problem is a world where everyone just falls in line and starts each day at eight o'clock in the morning. There's no rhyme or reason for this, other than the weak excuse of, "It's always been done that way!" Yeah, sure… that's the same weak excuse I was given whenever I questioned cold calling.

When I moved to Phoenix in 2000, the city's businesses were starved for broadband Internet service. I accepted a job offer from a wireless Internet startup, but they had no idea what they were doing (ironically, they're based in Dallas, where I later lived). I soon left and went to a small, local, self-funded competitor. It seemed like amateur night compared to the corporate world of the previous employer; however, their product simply worked! To me, that's the difference between a company that gets venture capital and is suddenly worried about what kind of handmade Italian desks to buy and a company that just bootstraps it and gets the job done.

Within about two months I was one of six sales reps, yet I was producing 50% of all of the company's sales volume. I soon became good friends with the one honest owner, and we remained friends. (The other two ripped off investors and got dragged through lawsuit after lawsuit. They also tanked the company, for which I'm grateful, since this was not long after 9/11, no one was hiring, and I was forced to start a business. Thanks, guys!)

Imagine that…a sudden quantum shift from a lifetime of struggle, unhappiness, and especially fatigue, to a life filled with abundance and success. All because I could sleep a couple of hours later!

Part of why I'm writing this book is because we're in the Internet-based Information Age and the days of forcing people to show up at an office at 8:00 a.m. are starting to wane. Sure, it's happening very slowly, but then again, that's why I'm writing this.

When employers come to realize that anywhere from a third to a half of their employees are night owls, and will perform better and reduce company turnover if they're allowed to work during their most productive hours, employers will make those changes and fewer people will experience the level of misery that I did.

When corporate wellness programs begin to customize employee profiles based on sleep habits, they'll be better able to customize the wellness program to each individual versus trying to force the same program on everyone. Wellness will improve and the employer's health insurance costs will drop. So will sick days.

When universities, for whom the all-important graduation rate is king (remember, they're all about money today and operate like businesses), come to understand and accept this knowledge, students will be able to create schedules that work for them. I fully believe that I'd have graduated college with honors had I been able to start the day at 10:00 or 11:00 a.m. Indeed, more and more private virtual universities—the ones that don't pretend that they're not businesses—are popping up. These are *real* university degrees that you can complete virtually on your own schedule. Southern New Hampshire University is perhaps the best known thanks to their heavy advertising, along with the many schools now offering online MBAs. Heck, even schools like Harvard offer virtual MBAs today.

Billionaire Mark Cuban, who lives nearby and whose neighborhood I drive through several times a week for inspiration, has been extremely vocal about the fact that higher education in America has turned into a scam, and predicts that traditional universities will be largely replaced by online universities as more and more people wise up and see what's happening. I mean seriously, outside of doctors and lawyers, I really can't think of many people who work in a field that's even remotely related to their college major. Talk about a giant waste of money. Granted, I wish I hadn't missed out on the social aspect of college, but for what it costs, I could put on the party to end all parties!

From the perspective of morning larks versus night owls, if Mr. Cuban is correct, that one change will totally transform higher education as we know it. Never mind the fact that costs will be slashed; the larger benefit is that the one-third to one-half of society who happen to be naturally born night owls will be able to participate and study on their own schedules, and that will make them *happy*, *successful*, and even *healthier* than being forced to conform to a morning-centric world.

Morning Madness

We live in a morning-centric society, where both the school day and the workday begin at around eight o'clock in the morning. This alienates and impairs the performance of the one-third to one-half of society who are night owls, and employers who force everyone to work on the same schedule are unknowingly losing money and productivity, while schools that do so are limiting their graduation rates along with their students' intellectual potential.

2

The Brainwashing

Society Stigmatizes Night Owls—and People Buy It

"Why isn't he up yet? No one should be in bed this late!"
"Never let the sun catch you in bed."
"Successful people are up before the sun every day."
"Night owls are lazy sloths!"

How many of these statements have you heard? I know that first one has been said about me many times. Anytime I visit family back in New Jersey or New York, whether it's my wife's or my own, it seems to be a running joke among everyone present that I sleep late.

I always dread walking down the stairs in the morning and hearing the snarky, "Well, gee whiz, rise and shine!" Or, "It's about time you got up." Or, "How can you have successful businesses when you're always sleeping?"

The Myth of Night Owl "Laziness"

As I write this, I can tell you that I went to bed slightly after 2:00 a.m. last night, and slept only five hours. Is that oversleeping? I don't think so—that's undersleeping! In fact, the only reason I only got five hours of sleep is because my wife and kids are away visiting her family in New York State, and our dog and cat wake me up every day to get fed. Normally my wife is up before six so I do get a good night's sleep most nights.

I typically get in seven to eight hours, which is the normal amount of time that human beings need to remain healthy and give the body enough time to rest, recover from the previous day, and get ready for the next. How is *that* "lazy" or "oversleeping"?

Here's the catch: Let's say I go to bed at 1:00 a.m., which is pretty typical for me. Then I get up at 9:00 a.m., also my usual time. That's a normal eight-hour sleep period.

However, to outside observers, they never see the work and thinking and planning and reading that happen late at night. You see, I never stop educating myself. Ever since I learned that most CEOs and even some U.S. presidents read a book a week, and always wanting to emulate those who are more successful than I, I've begun that habit as well. Even if I'm waiting somewhere, say at a car wash, I'll take out my phone, open the Kindle app, and continue reading a book. Or I'll review my goals and write them down again—a very effective habit that burns them into your mind more deeply than by merely reading them aloud.

Likewise, I never stop working. I'm not up past midnight watching movies. I'm up past midnight getting important shit done while the rest of the world sleeps.

My immediate family—my wife and kids—know that I work like crazy. When I'm not spending time exclusively with them, I nearly always have a laptop out doing work, day and night. My kids wonder why I sleep late, but then again they're too young to understand yet. (I do love it when I happen to wake up early and catch them before school; some days I'll get up to see them, then go back to bed for a couple more hours.) My wife totally gets it and has no problem with my habits. It was even an asset when we had babies—I'd stay up until 2:30 a.m. or so, then my wife would get up at 5:30 a.m. since she's a morning person. That worked perfectly—both babies slept during the time in between and we both got a full night's rest in, every night!

I honestly don't understand how couples who are on the same sleep schedule survive having babies. But then again, I vividly remember working with new dads who would come into work with bags under their eyes that were so dark, they looked like raccoons. How they managed to be productive under those circumstances is beyond me. There's no possible way their work output and quality didn't suffer.

Society's Negative Attitudes Toward Night Owls

Those quotes at the beginning of this chapter, the kind that I've had to listen to all my life and learn to take in stride and ignore, represent very typical attitudes that the majority of Western people hold against night owls.

A quick Google search of quotes about the virtues of being a morning person turned up endless results. That alone goes to show that society has been brainwashed to believe that we should continue to follow work schedules that were created hundreds of years ago for the purpose of farming, and continue to use them in our modern Internet- and data-driven economy.

Here's some of the nonsense I found looking for those quotes:

Work hard, stay positive, and get up early. It's the best part of the day.

—George Allen, Sr.

My response: No, it's not. It's a miserable time of day for a night owl to be up.

The early bird gets the worm. The early worm … gets eaten.

—Norman Ralph Augustine

My response: *Wrong*! Science shows that while the early bird might catch the worm, he cannot go the distance; only night owls can. You'll learn why in a subsequent chapter. Morning people crash just when night owls are getting warmed up.

Formula for success: rise early, work hard, strike oil.

—J. Paul Getty

My response: That's easy to say when you've already struck oil, especially when you can do that any time of day. Oil doesn't show up early in the morning and then disappear into the night. Drilling at two o'clock in the morning will get the same result as drilling at six o'clock, just like all work product will be the same regardless of what time of day it's done.

Lose an hour in the morning, and you will be all day hunting for it.

—Richard Whately

My response: What is that? Funny math? There are twenty-four hours in every day. That never changes. We all get the same twenty-four hours. Instead of wasting that hour in the morning when I'm groggy and useless, I save it for my most productive and creative time: night. I have no problem with you being an early riser, but don't try to force it on me.

And of course we cannot forget my all-time favorite, the one that was disproven by folks who knew Mr. Franklin. By his own admission, Franklin got up at 9:00 a.m. every day despite living in times with no electric lights, when people naturally got up with the sunrise:

Early to bed and early to rise makes a man healthy, wealthy, and wise.

—Benjamin Franklin

Personally, I think that's the most damaging of all early-bird quotes for the simple fact that it's the most well known. Think about it: Can you think of any adults you know who haven't heard that quote, or even recited it themselves? Even children are exposed to that nonsense in school.

Here's the thing about Benjamin Franklin: He's one of America's Founding Fathers and I will always have the utmost respect for Mr. Franklin, especially since I've been to Philadelphia several times where I've visited multiple museums and exhibits about the life of Benjamin Franklin. He truly accomplished a lot, and even the size of his house is seriously impressive, even compared with modern housing!

Having said all that, Mark Twain's grandfather happened to be friends with Ben Franklin, and told Samuel Clemens just how much Franklin was a "Do as I say, not as I do" sort of fellow.

For example, Franklin preached and wrote endlessly about the virtue of being industrious and never wasting time on activities that don't produce anything for you in return. But Mark Twain's granddad constantly found Franklin frittering away his time playing games by himself and doing other useless activities that are typical of procrastinators.

Most important of all, by Ben Franklin's own admission, he got up at 9:00 a.m. every day. Now I get shit from people, today in the twenty-first century, when I get up at nine! Back in colonial days, that was extremely late; there was no artificial lighting and most people arose at daylight. Considering that sunrise generally happens on average at between 6 and 6:30 a.m., Franklin was very likely a major-league night owl by comparison with his peers!

Perhaps that was the secret of his success?

However, this "early rising" nonsense is what society has been brainwashed to believe. Or I should say, has been *led* to believe by morons who don't know what they're talking about.

Here's a good example of the kind of damage morons can do: I got to know the brother of a very famous and wealthy person who lives nearby. His degree is in law—he's an attorney by trade—yet he claims to be an expert on addiction. However, everything he teaches entirely contradicts the method I used to quit drinking. It has a documented 90% success rate versus the 96% *failure* rate of Alcoholics Anonymous. Anytime I bring it up with him, he goes "shields up" and shuts down the conversation. This is despite the fact that he's invested as much as 12 years "in recovery," as he calls it. He's still resisting the craving for a drink—for over a decade—and continues to commence his monologue with, "I am an alcoholic," while the methodology I used completely removed the desire for alcohol. Indeed, not only do I never crave a drink, but also the thought of having one is revolting, and the few times I have since had a drink under peer pressure, I did not enjoy it at all. Interestingly, I didn't get hooked again either, despite what Alcoholics Anonymous would have you believe, which is the exact opposite.

So, what did I do? I had a conversation with my very expensive, exclusive, noninsurance concierge doctor, one of the best in town. He explained in detail why everything my friend's brother is saying about addiction is not only medical mythology, but it's keeping alcoholics and other addicts stuck in the trap. In other words, it's complete bullshit coming from a guy trying to sell his books on addiction and recovery.

Needless to say, I no longer waste my time trying to convince that lawyer who plays fake doctor for a living that he is wrong. In fact, I don't bother speaking with him at all anymore. The reason I brought it up, however, is because his mindset is exactly like those who still claim that early rising is the key to success. Worse yet are all the self-righteous morning people, who all seem to have a chip on their shoulder about it and cannot mention the fact that they get up early without also sounding like "Aren't I a goody-goody?"

In my books on sales—for example, *Never Cold Call Again: Achieve Sales Greatness Without Cold Calling* (Wiley, 2006)—I obliterate the myths about how cold calling works and teach sales professionals alternative methods of generating leads, methods that actually work in today's high-tech society in which decision makers wall themselves off using gatekeepers, fake voicemail boxes that salesmen are transferred to (and which are never checked), and on and on.

Likewise, in this book my goal is to obliterate the myths and the societal disapproval of night owls by proving that we are more successful, more productive, more creative, and generally more prosperous than morning larks.

How People Fall into the Morning Trap

This concept of always getting up at sunrise, or never letting the sun catch you in bed, was literally invented about 10,000 years ago for the purpose of farming.

I'm totally serious … and we're still using that ancient work schedule today in the Information Age!

You see, the economic transition to agriculture, or the birth of the Agrarian Age, happened sometime between 8,000 and 10,000 years ago in the Fertile Crescent region of the Middle East. Farming and agriculture also appeared around 6,800 BC in East Asia, where rice was farmed, and also in Central and South America (maize and squash, initially). Rice farming also likely arose in India around the same time, and taro agriculture began in Southeast Asia.

Fast-forward, oh, 10,000 years or so, and we end up in the late 1800s, 1870 specifically, and people were still living in the Agrarian Age, earning both a living and subsistence by farming. At that time the average workweek was between 60 and 70 hours. (So stop complaining when you have to work a little overtime!)

Fast-forward to today and the average workweek has dropped to around 38 hours per week. In other words, we're down to a point where we are working not much more than half the hours that people worked only a century prior. In the United States, the average workweek is only 33.9 hours! Heck, even in my lifetime that used to be considered part-time. As it turns out, the wealthier the country, the fewer hours citizens work on average.

So, based on that, why on earth are people still getting up at the crack of dawn when this incredible drop in weekly working hours has occurred? There's no reason to be up before dawn in an era when few people still farm and workweeks are nowhere near 70 hours. Especially when, here in the United States at least, that number is down to 33.9 hours.

To further put things in perspective, in Germany the average workweek is 26.4 hours, and in the United Kingdom it's only 32.2 hours a week.

Now granted, this hyperproductive, "never let the sun catch you in bed" attitude is largely an American phenomenon. So is the destructive habit of downing massive amounts of coffee all day. When my sister got married, she and her husband went on a honeymoon to Italy and were shocked at how small a cup of coffee is over there. That's because they know how to live well in Italy, they're not up at five o'clock in the morning, and as a result they don't need to pump their bodies full of caffeine, a dangerous habit that routinely results in adrenal fatigue. I'll talk more about that later in the book and how following the advice of another book that preaches the virtues of getting up at four or five in the morning actually made me physically ill. (Please, if you really intend to follow a program like that, see your doctor first and get your thyroid and adrenal function checked. Trust me on this: you don't want to experience the incredible level of exhaustion that I did, along with the business, financial, and even marital problems that having zero energy caused. You sure as hell won't want to experience that, after learning more about what happened to me.)

Even if downing coffee all day long doesn't cause adrenal problems for you as it did for me, what's the use of getting up so early in the first place that you even need coffee? Or to drink it only to experience a crash later on, rather than get the full amount of sleep that your particular body requires?

When I get a good night's sleep and I'm well rested, I don't bother with caffeine. Sure, I still drink coffee when I feel like I need it, but I keep it in moderation, just like they do in Italy, knowing that having too much of a caffeine rush will result in an equally large crash later on, and also knowing that it takes about two hours to reach peak effectiveness; anyone who suddenly brightens up as soon as they sip their first coffee of the day is experiencing a placebo effect.

This is contrary to the incorrect societal belief that we night owls must survive on coffee because we go to bed too late!

The late comedian George Carlin once said that the more complicated the Starbucks order, the bigger the asshole that is ordering it. "If you walk into a Starbucks and order a 'decaf grandee, half soy, half low fat, iced vanilla, double-shot, gingerbread cappuccino, extra dry, light ice, with one Sweet'n Low and one NutraSweet,' oooh, you're a huge asshole." (That's Carlin talking, not me.)

Guess who places Starbucks orders like that? You guessed it—those goody-goody morning people. While most are nice people, far too many have a superiority complex about getting up early, and it shows, with that Starbucks quote from Carlin being a prime example. Indeed, back in the bad old days of having to get up early to go to work, I learned to avoid Starbucks and go to Dunkin' Donuts or an independent coffee shop to avoid all those assholes holding up the line for a half hour, while always making a point to give everyone around them dirty looks as they hand the coffee back and demand that it's redone "right" this time. Ironically, in high-end coffee shops, where everything is truly gourmet, people simply order off the menu; there's no "half this, half that, light ice" nonsense happening there.

The Cult of the Early Riser

One thing I've noticed about the seeming cult of early risers is that it has very much the same characteristics of religious fanaticism.

For example, they'll tell you all those quotes about why getting up early makes them so great, yet they can't explain why. In other words, they're just going on faith. In other words, they've come to believe the brainwashing.

Likewise, if you ask someone why they are a member of a particular religion, or why they vote for a particular political party, they will invariably tell you, "Because that's what my parents did."

That's not much of a choice, is it? Like I said, early rising and the cult of morning people resembles religious fanaticism and taking advice on blind faith, rather than employing logic and reason. I was born in a working-class Democratic family and then became a Republican in my teens, thanks to educating myself on what both sides stand for. I didn't blindly follow my parents; in fact I converted them, as well.

Reading the autobiographies of countless successful men and women, I've seen that one common theme is that their fathers drilled early rising into their heads.

In Conrad Hilton's *Be My Guest* (Fireside, 1984), which I got for free when Hilton hotels used to put a free copy in every room, he wrote that he started his habit of getting up at 5:00 a.m. every day after he slept in until 7:00 a.m. one day. He overheard his father freaking out, saying something like "The boy will never amount to anything unless he gets up before dawn." Mr. Hilton took that advice on blind faith and got up at five in the morning for the rest of his life.

Likewise, Clarence Thomas, in *My Grandfather's Son: A Memoir* (Harper, 2007), writes that his grandfather taught him never to let the sun catch him in bed, and he never did again.

Granted, these are very successful men. Having said that, the majority of people are not night owls; that's why they don't like us. It's common for the majority to be suspicious and afraid of the minority, which is exactly what happens to night owls, and make no mistake, night owls are discriminated against equally as bad, or worse, than other minority groups. Indeed, I've been mocked and criticized for being a late riser by people of almost every race and sexual orientation you can think of.

Based on that, common sense says that both of those men were natural morning people. If they were not, I can guarantee you that they'd never have survived habits such as getting up at 5:00 a.m. or being up before sunrise. Then again, Justice Thomas looks older than he actually is, and just looking at what happens to the face of any American president over eight years is proof of how insufficient sleep greatly accelerates the aging process.

It reminds me of the antiracism movie *Blazing Saddles*, when Bart said, "I don't know. But whatever it is, I hate it." Morning people may not necessarily hate us, but far too many see us as inferior, or lazy, or just plain "different," as though we should be riding the short bus to work.

It makes one wonder just how many successful people were given advice like that, found that it didn't work, and went on to huge success as night owls.

This is the brainwashing I'm talking about.

You see, in a cult, members don't read the Bible or learn about a legitimate religious faith. What happens in a cult is that members are brainwashed to blindly follow the leader.

Likewise, people who are told to get up early, without any explanation or science to support why they should do so, are taking that advice on blind faith, with no rhyme or reason, just like a cult member.

Modern society continues to bombard us with this idea that early rising is virtuous while there's something wrong or even sinful about getting up later than average.

In an article on Vox.com entitled "Late sleepers are tired of being discriminated against. And science has their back," Brian Resnick writes that late sleepers are made to feel like losers.

While he points out that night owls merely have a different internal clock and sleep on a different schedule, they're commonly perceived as partiers, deadbeats, irresponsible, and unable to keep a schedule.

He goes on to interview a few night owls, and the responses he received are extremely eye opening:

"They just thought I was a fuck-up," one woman said about her parents' opinion of her natural night owl tendencies. In her family, early rising was expected. She went on to say that she ended up taking strong stimulants in the morning to function during the day, and then consumed excessive amounts of alcohol at night to counter the stimulants and get to sleep. I went through the same nasty cycle every day when I had jobs that required me to be in the office early. Back then I'd get myself to sleep with several glasses of wine, then use ephedrine and coffee to wake up; that's anything but healthy.

This is the kind of damage that society's attitudes toward night owls cause. The woman interviewed for the Vox article was not only fired from a job for sleeping late too many times, but was forced to become a drug addict and alcoholic just to try to conform to society's working hours—the same schedule the world has been using for 10,000 years. (I mean, come on—that right there tells you it's time for a change already!)

I myself drank excessively for several years, and part of the reason was to fall asleep early enough in order to get up early. Needless to say, it didn't work.

A student at Northern Arizona University said, "People have mocked me for it, saying how lazy I am, that I'm not trying hard enough, and that really bothers me, because it's not my fault. I'm really, really trying, and it's just not working."

Of course it's not working; that's not her natural schedule. She went on to say that she saw a doctor, who told her to stop drinking coffee and she'd be fine. (How?)

Amy, a Seattle night owl, said, "There's a lot of emotional baggage tied up into going to work. You're arriving later, you feel like you're not actually present, when people ask you questions, you give stupid answers."

Oh, how I feel her pain, because I've been there too, and I have a feeling you have as well, since you're reading this book, a book that I've been writing from 1:00 p.m. to 6:00 p.m. every day because those are my peak hours.

Enough is enough already. It's time for society to become more accepting and accommodating of the one-third to one-half of those of us who are night owls.

In a world where the Internet allows people to work whenever, wherever, there is no reason for companies to continue to push the morning myth brainwashing.

Likewise, there's no reason to force a night owl student—and most are night owls at college age—to be in a lecture hall at 8:00 a.m. when he or she can view a recording of it online later in the day.

Morning Madness

Society is stuck on a work schedule created 10,000 years ago for the purpose of maximizing farming output. Members of society, particularly early risers themselves, continue to brainwash people that getting up early is the key to success and happiness, when in reality, following your own internal clock is the real key to success and happiness. The endless brainwashing we're exposed to even convinces millions of night owls to attempt to become morning people, frequently with disastrous results, as was the case with me.

CHAPTER

3

The Prison

How Our Society's Discrimination Harms Night Owls

I called the endless garbage society pushes on us, described in Chapter 2, as "the brainwashing," because even night owls come to believe this nonsense that early rising is an absolute essential to success in school and in life.

I know I certainly did, and for a long time I thought there was something medically wrong with me. I read endless books on chronic fatigue syndrome, high-energy diets, and much, much more. My wife will tell you I love reading medical books and over the past few years I've learned so much that I can even talk to doctors in medical terms. I remember being in agony the morning after my ankle surgery, saying, "It's on the medial side!" "Are you sure you don't mean lateral?" "No, I mean medial ..."

I was born with hypothyroidism—low thyroid function, which causes chronic fatigue—but I'd been taking Armour Thyroid® replacement hormone, desiccated pig thyroid, and my thyroid labs were at normal levels, so that wasn't it.

Eventually I simply gave up. I had accepted the brainwashing. I accepted my fate as being a night owl and settled for a life of believing that the problem was with me, not with society's celebratory views on early rising.

At that point, I was fully locked up in "the prison."

The definition of the prison is the life of the night owl who is forced to live in a world where schedules are dictated by early risers. It makes them feel ashamed, inferior, and not a productive member of society. Worse, many night owls assume there must be something wrong with them, that they must indeed be lazy, slothful, and disorganized.

When the night owl tries to switch to an early-riser sleep schedule, the result is cognitive impairment, reduced productivity, higher risk of causing an automobile accident while driving to work, and more. Perhaps the worst consequence is the inability to hold onto a job. I know I went through this early in my sales career, having to fight traffic in an hour-long commute to arrive at a daily 7:30 a.m. sales meeting on time. Heck, I even lost my job as an auto mechanic after leaving school because I had trouble getting there by 8:00 a.m., even though the shop was 10 minutes from home. Mind you I was only 20 years old at the time, young enough to have been bursting with energy, but that didn't help me to get up any earlier.

That is also largely why I failed at so many sales jobs, despite having strong sales skills. When I was hired by the person I call

"my first sales manager with a brain," I no longer had to show up
at 8:00 a.m. for daily meetings or just for the sake of being there.
While it's true that his sharing the fact that cold calling is a waste
of time really did skyrocket my sales career, a big part of my success was that I no longer had to get up at 5:30 or 6:00 a.m. to get
to work on time. As long as I was producing sales numbers—and
I was—he didn't care if I slept in until noon and played golf
every day. (Yes, he actually said that. But I hate golf.) So, I got up
at my normal time of between 8:30 and 9:00 a.m. and suddenly
I was "on"—wired, ambitious, prepared to conquer the world.
And at that job, I did; in fact, it was the success and knowledge
gained working there that allowed me to save enough money
to start a business, and only three years later my first book was
released and immediately became a *New York Times* best-seller.
Keep in mind this was three years of being my own boss and,
most important, sleeping on my own schedule. Most of that
book, and all of my others, was written while all those lazy-ass
morning people were in bed sleeping. (See how easily we can
turn it around on them?)

As you can see, that job was anything but a prison; however,
the overwhelming majority of night owls are stuck in 8-to-5 jobs,
or in school with similar early hours, which means getting up as
early as six o'clock in the morning to get there on time. Many
employers are beginning to allow flexible hours but we have a
long, long way to go. I don't think society will ever stop believing
Ben Franklin's blatant lie about rising early, written at the same
time that he was waking up at nine o'clock every day.

In his book *Why We Sleep* (Scribner, 2017), Dr. Matthew
Walker explains that about 40% of the population are morning
people, 30% are night owls, and the remaining 30% fall somewhere in between.

This means that *less than half of society consists of morning people*,
yet everyone has to fall in line in the same prison nevertheless.

He goes on to say that when night owls are forced to rise early, the prefrontal cortex in the brain, which controls thought processes and logical reasoning, remains in a disabled or "offline" state. "Like a cold engine in an early-morning start, it takes a long time before it warms up to operating temperature."

I can't speak for anyone else, but I take about two hours from waking to feeling fully alert. Having said that, two hours is the average time for *all* people to become fully alert after getting out of bed. It's no coincidence, then, that a disproportionate amount of automobile accidents occur during the morning commute. To further complicate matters, most people get up and immediately start drinking coffee, usually more than one cup. And when I say cup, I mean a normal cup like you get in a diner, not a giant Starbucks coffee or a huge travel mug filled to the brim; that's more like three or four cups. As Stephen Cherniske explains in his book *Caffeine Blues: Wake Up to the Hidden Dangers of America's #1 Drug* (Grand Central Publishing, 2008), the hyper state that caffeine induces contributes to morning road rage, excessive speeding and weaving in and out of traffic, and overall aggressive driving, all of which lead to even more car accidents in the morning hours. The frantic rush to get to work at a too-early hour contributes as well.

While I'm rarely on the road during morning rush hour, the few times I am, which are mostly for school events, I am stunned at just how aggressive, obnoxious, and angry drivers seem to be, supporting Cherniske's claims. It's also very interesting to note that I don't experience this when I drive home during afternoon rush hour, which is typically when I head home. I have to believe that's because everyone isn't hyped up on caffeine and making a mad rush to get to work on time. (It's a sad state of affairs, however, if people aren't rushing home to see their families. I know

I do, or perhaps I'm unknowingly using that to justify my high rate of speed?)

By the way, after reading *Caffeine Blues* and weaning myself off of coffee, I amazingly did start waking up earlier and just as refreshed as if I'd slept until 10:00 a.m., which was my normal time for most of my life. Being caffeine-free has pushed that back to between 8:30 and 9:00 a.m. I personally believe it is the one and only thing that will help night owls get up earlier, but wean yourself slowly by gradually mixing in decaf with your regular coffee over a month until you're drinking strictly decaf, which still contains caffeine, at which point you can safely quit without the brutal withdrawal headaches associated with caffeine cessation. Oh, and when I say get up earlier, you won't be jumping out of bed at 5:30 a.m. The difference will be more like 30–60 minutes earlier. Interestingly, the reason for caffeine withdrawal headaches is because caffeine is a vasoconstrictor, meaning it narrows your blood vessels. After years of drinking coffee, then stopping, the blood vessels to your brain are no longer constricted and can finally function normally, and it's the new flood of oxygen into the brain that triggers the headaches. Or, in other words, caffeine limits the amount of oxygen your brain gets, literally making you dumber. Until you quit, anyway.

In other words, consuming caffeine, especially in large amounts, is tantamount to going from the town jail to the state penitentiary.

I can say with certainty that quitting alcohol had little positive impact, and in fact it had negative ones such as gaining weight just like smokers do when they quit; dropping caffeine, on the other hand, was almost miraculous in terms of how much more energy I suddenly had! Even my wife, who has known me for over 14 years, said one day, "Who are you?" (That's one of my favorite songs by the way—and she hates it!)

Morning People Can't Keep Their Mouths Shut About It

As part of the research for this book, I came across an article in the *New York Times* by Alex Williams, entitled *Maybe Your Sleep Problem Isn't a Problem*.

He recalls being on a Delta airlines flight and seeing one of their commercials from his in-seat screen, one that hits home a bit too hard for us night owls:

It starts off with a montage of perky professionals, rising before dawn in homes and executive-class hotel rooms around the world, stretching their gym-toned bodies and firing up coffeepots at an hour usually reserved for mating fruit bats.

"Here's to all 180 million of you early risers, go-getters and should-be sleepers," the voice-over says, as Disney's "Heigh-Ho" swells in the background. "Because the ones who truly change the world are the ones who can't wait to get out in it."

All that commercials like this do is to reinforce the myth that morning people are more punctual (not in my experience, while I'm never, ever late), and do better in school and in their careers. Society continues to celebrate these so-called winners, and despite all the research to the contrary, commercials like Delta's and other media continue to perpetuate this myth that morning people are just somehow *better*, and that night owls are losers.

As you'll learn throughout this book, the truth is the exact opposite: *Night owls are more successful and earn more money than morning people.*

If you doubt that statement, consider someone like Mark Zuckerberg, who routinely stays up until 6:00 a.m. Love him or hate him, he is a very well-known—and very wealthy—night owl and, like me, has no shame about it.

Then there's former U.S. president Barack Obama. Even during his two terms as president, he went to bed at 1:00 a.m. and started work at 9:00 a.m.... and despite that—or perhaps because of it—he went on to achieve the highest level of success on this side of the pond—President of the United States of America.

Or consider the man who saved England from Germany during World War II. Winston Churchill got up at 11, started work at noon, and required his staff to work as late as he did. Hah—take *that*, you early risers!

If Jerry Seinfeld weren't a night owl, he wouldn't have been able to spend years working late-night comedy clubs and would not have a current net worth estimated at $870 million. Yes, you heard that right—he's close to becoming a *billionaire*—all thanks to the ability to be sharp late at night. (Don't think a morning person can just hammer coffee and be equally sharp at that hour; as you're about to learn in the upcoming chapters, they simply cannot, just as we cannot be expected to be that "on" in the early mornings.)

Having said all that, in my research for this book, I found article after article claiming that these, and many other highly successful night owls, are actually morning people! The nerve! Or, I should say, the brainwashing.

Maybe they're not brainwashed. Maybe they're night owls, too, but their employers are making them write this drivel to fulfill their superiority complex over late risers.

Night Owl Shaming Must Stop—*Now*

Throughout my life, as you know, I've been a night owl. Even when I have the best intentions of going to bed early, it simply does not happen, no matter how tired I am.

Just recently I was seriously exhausted after a lousy night's sleep the night before. I went to bed about two hours earlier than my usual time, expecting to be asleep by the time my head hit the pillow.

An hour later I gave up and got back up.

While my wife understands it, even my kids, at five and seven years old, ask me why I sleep "so late." It doesn't help much to try to explain it when they are in a world where mommy gets to work and they get to school at eight o'clock, just as I'm getting close to waking up.

In fact, friends, relatives, and other successful people will shame me. Coworkers did it when I had a job, and during my one year in college—which I flunked out of thanks to the eight o'clock start—friends would try to come and wake me up to get me to class, but it was to no avail. When I visit family out of state it's like some kind of running joke that I get up as late as I do. Then again, my brother Dan and sister Lisa also get up late, thanks to the genetic nature of sleep chronotypes. More on that later.

We live in a politically correct society where shaming someone for their race or gender or sexual orientation can get you thrown in jail on hate speech charges, yet it's somehow okay to shame night owls. The problem is especially enormous in America, where the myth of the "successful early riser and lazy night owl" persists, and on top of that, countries in Europe, South America, and elsewhere have gotten with the program and it's common for employers there to offer flexible hours to late risers.

Camilla Kring, the founder of *B-Society*, a night owl advocacy group, says that the typical workday discriminates against late-sleeping night owls.

"Early risers have the competitive edge. Most schools and workplaces are organized based on an 8:00 or 9:00 o'clock starting time. But why are we considered less productive if we prefer an active evening and calm morning? And why do early risers have the patent on discipline simply because they get up early? Quality of life, health, infrastructure, and productivity would all improve if we offered people work hours matching their circadian rhythms."

Silicon Valley is a prime example. It's one of the most expensive places to live in America, has many of the most desirable jobs, and—drumroll please—is the one place in the United States where flexible work schedules are offered to accommodate early risers, night owls, and everyone in between.

Why can't the rest of America get off their early morning high horse and get with *that* program? After all, are they not aware of the fact that the area has an annual GDP of approximately one trillion dollars? Yes, that's trillion with a capital T, more than most countries. Here's a new slogan for them: "Silicon Valley—Where Night Owls Can Be Night Owls."

As Silicon Valley continues to migrate from Northern California to North Texas (the Dallas area), hopefully they bring their positive attitudes toward night owls with them and we can finally be done with this Southern nonsense of everyone being in a pissing contest to see who gets bragging rights about being the earliest riser of all. I've literally heard conversations like this: "I get up at 5:30 every day." "Well I'm up at five." "Heck, I'm up at 4:30." And it's not just Texas; I heard this kind of stupidity living in Arizona, Nevada, and other states.

Biologist Christoph Randler, interviewed in the July–August 2010 issue of *Harvard Business Review*, was challenged on the accuracy of his research showing that early risers do better in life than night owls.

However, when pressed on the issue, he said, "Children show a marked increase in eveningness from around age 13 to late adolescence, and, on balance, more people under 30 are evening types. From 30 to 50, the population is about evenly split, but after age 50, most people are morning types."

Guess who the business owners and CEOs primarily are? If you guessed the over-50 crowd, you guessed right, although I still question even that statement. I'm in my late 40s and not even remotely close to somehow magically transforming into a morning person. All age has given me is multiple pairs of reading glasses that I keep everywhere. Granted, I only need them when I'm tired and the fatigue blurs my near-field vision, but still…

Here's another admission from Mr. Randler that contradicts his claims about the superiority of early risers and the idea that people can change their sleep schedule: "Throughout the world, people who sleep late are too often assumed to be lazy. The result is that the vast majority of school and work schedules are tailored to morning types. Few people are even aware that morningness and eveningness have a powerful biological component."

There you have it, thanks to an evidently anonymous interviewer at HBR: We're assumed to be lazy throughout the world, yet few people are aware that our night owl tendencies are inherited and biological, and they cannot be changed. *Society must change to better accommodate* us.

It's no wonder why night owls have higher rates of depression and anxiety, when society demeans us and demands that we conform to ancient agrarian work and school schedules. Then they have the nerve to call us lazy and slothful when we don't. I'm sorry, but if that's not discrimination, then I don't know what is.

Perhaps the time has come for lawyers to get in on this? After all, the opioid crisis in America has fueled an unexpected cottage industry: malpractice lawsuits against doctors who do not provide adequate pain relief to those in need of it, something that I personally experienced and that led to my heavy drinking for pain relief and the ability to sleep through pain. The worst part was when I had a total ankle replacement last year and the

IV pain medications were not working because all that booze made my liver extremely efficient at removing toxins. I ended up on hydromorphone, which is four times more powerful than heroin, and oral oxycodone on top of that, and yet I was still in agony. After all, my bones had been power-sawed, drilled, and had metal implants hammered into them the previous day. That hurts!

Likewise, looking back on those years of, one, suffering through extremely difficult mornings when I couldn't think straight, let alone perform, and two, the endless sleep shaming from seemingly everyone, I think we're long overdue for *something* to change in our society.

I'll close this chapter with a quote from author Chelsea Fagan, in an article in *Thought Catalog*:

All I ask is that morning people be kind to night owls, that they try their best to understand how difficult life already is in the first few hours of the day and not compound it with suggestions on how to perk up and loud monologues about all of the things they've already accomplished. When I am just sipping a coffee and trying to get acclimated to human life, and someone comes up and starts talking at me, it's all I can do not to just pour my coffee on them and burst into tears. Don't do that. Be kind. Be chill. Above all, be the kind of person that night owls want to invite to their sweet-ass parties, because you know we're throwing all of them.

Morning Madness

Society's endless insistence on early morning schedules along with the endless shaming of night owls is literally a form of discrimination that must be stopped. How many millions of night owls must suffer what I suffered: Daily wondering of what's wrong with me, why I can't get up early and perform well, and being sick and tired of early risers shaming us and then telling us just how wonderful their mornings are, complete with a snarky, "Nice of you to join us today" when we do arrive. Enough is enough already. Bring on the lawyers.

4

Studies Favoring Morning Larks Are Fatally Flawed

Our Society Is Rigged in Favor of Early Birds

A t this point I've ranted and raved relentlessly (say that fast 10 times) about the fact that night owls are forced to live, learn, and work in a world that's still ruled by a centuries-old, farming-centric school and work schedule.

Take today, for instance. I got up 10 minutes before my wife and kids left for the day. As much as I hate getting up at 7:30 a.m., which snarky morning people will laugh at and consider to be very late, I do try to see my kids every day. They're disappointed when I don't, although I have a much clearer head on days that I sleep until my usual time. If I do get up even earlier, I'll go back to bed for another hour or two before getting on with my day.

If researchers were to single me out and ask me to participate in a study comparing the performance and success of night owls with morning larks, I'd jump at the chance—*if* I knew it were going to be a fair study.

By fair study I mean one that measures participants at all times of day—morning, midday, and night.

However, few do that. Hence the popular myth and the endless articles on websites, blogs, and in business and personal productivity publications touting studies showing that early risers perform better at work and school while night owls fall far behind in performance.

Well, of course early risers do better at work and at school; that's because these are activities that, save for nighttime jobs like bartender or police officer, mostly start at eight o'clock in the morning, or nine o'clock if you're lucky, at least here in the United States, although in my experience work times are trending earlier, not later. American employers just can't seem to get past Ben Franklin's lie.

As a night owl I had to drag myself through school, began to see my grades decline in the latter half of high school, then flunked out of college because I couldn't get myself to classes on time. It's pretty tough to pass exams when you missed all the lectures and before everyone had a smartphone to record them! This is why I believe Mark Cuban is right when he says that people now realize that a high-priced four-year university degree is a scam and does not show a positive return on investment anymore. Online universities are going to gradually replace traditional universities as people continue to ask why they're spending 40 grand a year to go to schools that have massive endowments. Or, I should say, go into debt at a rate of 40 grand a year, then find that their degree is worthless because everyone else has one, too.

I ended up chatting with someone at Starbucks one day; he was working on his Harvard MBA, remotely. Now that's the way to do it!

The other big standout about online universities is that there's no dragging yourself out of bed to wake up, make some coffee, shower, get dressed and ready for the day, all before having to arrive for an 8:00 a.m. class. Online, you can do it at your own pace. In fact our summer nanny told me that she learned Spanish online from Dallas County Community College.

But I digress. Those studies that you'll find all over the Internet with a quick Google search state that morning larks do better at work and school because work and school start early.

Night owls are effectively down for the count when the study measures performance in the morning. That doesn't sound very scientific to me. As a science nerd, anytime a doctor prescribes me anything, I read up on it before taking it, and I especially love reading about the pharmacology of drugs. In fact I've read books on the topic just for the sheer hell of it.

And when I read those studies, I can see that they're done as double-blind, placebo-controlled studies. That means both the real drug and the fake one, a sugar pill, are manufactured to look identical, and what's more, even the doctors administering the drugs don't know which is which or who is getting what. Hence the term "double-blind."

When it comes to studies on morning larks versus night owls, the studies aren't very scientific at all. Oh wait, I'm getting ahead of myself here. I'm going to cite studies that are in fact fair and accurate, but you'll find that if you do your own research, most are heavily biased toward morning people.

In an article in the July–August 2010 issue of *Harvard Business Review*, biologist Christoph Randler defends his research showing that morning people perform better at university.

How did he conduct his "research"? He *asked* 367 university students what time of day they perform best. (How does someone get into *Harvard Business Review* with that garbage? I suppose whoever chose to publish that has a morning person superiority complex.)

That is not scientific whatsoever, and I'll explain why in a moment. But let's get back to Mr. Randler's nonsense for now.

Mr. Randler said, "My earlier research showed that they tend to get better grades in school, which get them into better colleges, which then lead to better job opportunities."

There's proof of what I've been saying all along: Society discriminates against night owls, and Randler just explained why.

If someone is born a morning lark—and your circadian rhythm is something you are born with and that cannot be changed—they automatically get to sail down Easy Street, do well in school, and get into better colleges and get better jobs.

This isn't because there's anything essentially smarter or better about them. It's simply because society hands them a "get out of jail free" card when it comes to school and work performance—and even the prospect of getting a good job.

Randler also says morning people are more proactive; however, when challenged by the evidently anonymous interviewer, Randler admits that it's a simplification to say that morning people are more proactive. Well of course it is, Mr. Randler. Your study is not a study at all. He also claims that people can shift their sleep schedule, which is incorrect. It's possible to change it for a time, but it'll catch up with you rather quickly and you'll be back to bed late and getting up late.

Pushed further on his claims that morning people are more proactive than night owls, he admits that being proactive has a large genetic component to it. In other words, that's also something we're born with and cannot easily change.

When asked if companies will one day have to accommodate night-owl employees, something I'm advocating for along with B-Society, he says, "Morning people are very capable of understanding the value of chronotype diversity. *Remember, we're conscientious.*" (Emphasis mine.)

Oh yes, that's right. You get up at 5:00 a.m. and get right to work, and somehow that makes you more conscientious. Silly me, a worthless, lazy night owl, for not recognizing your superiority over us. Must I bow down to you, master?

When I mentioned earlier that his research method was simply asking a few hundred students what time of day they perform best, that was not scientific at all. I happen to know Dr. John Lott, author of *Freedomnomics: Why the Free Market Works and Other Half-Baked Theories Don't* (Regnery Publishing, 2007). As a career economist and statistical analyst, he uses very complex methods to come to his conclusions. These include mathematical models that may be the Tobit model, the probit model, generalized linear model, and many more.

In any case, these models use very complex mathematics to arrive at conclusions and also use large sample sizes. In other words, walking around a campus with a clipboard asking students when they perform best, with a very small sample size, and without running the answers through proper statistical analysis, is garbage. And for all we know he did it in the morning when the morning larks were out and about. His study—more like survey—does not note any times of day, making it even less reliable and believable.

In a Google search of the phrase "morning people do better at work," one of the first articles that came up is based on—wait for it—Randler's unscientific study. An article on Lifehack.com by David K. William cites Randler's "research" to claim that morning people are more proactive, despite the fact that Randler, when pushed, admitted that proactivity is largely biological.

The same article also claims that morning people are less prone to bad habits and drug abuse; however, there's no additional research to determine if night owls are more inclined toward drug abuse and alcoholism because of the difficulty and discrimination we experience living in a morning-centric society. At least that's what I believe based on my own experience—the bad old days of drinking a whole bottle of wine to get to sleep early, then chugging endless coffee in the morning to try and fight through the fog.

It also claims that morning people procrastinate less, because night owls push things off to the evening to get done. Well, that's when our brains light up and get to work. It's *not* procrastination. It's merely a different schedule, but, like all people guilty of discrimination, a fear of something different spurs reactions like this.

And finally, he says that morning people tend to be happier. However, he does admit that this may be largely due to the fact that night owls continually experience a disconnect between their natural sleep cycles and society's morning expectations. Yes, he's right—I was unhappy having to get up early every day. This is why I was hell-bent on never having a job again, and I achieved that goal back in 2003.

The article ends with, "For morning people, everything is as it should be. Morning people are happy with the typical day's schedule." That sounds to me like a frank admission that society puts night owls at a distinct disadvantage and that we suffer in many ways as a result.

More Morning Garbage from Leading Business Publications

Fast Company, which ironically named me one of the top 30 most influential people online even though I'm a night owl, published an article by Stephanie Vozza about why getting up early and becoming a morning person will make you better at your job.

˙ Let's tear this one apart, point by point:

> **"You Have More Energy."** Maybe natural early risers do, but I'm useless for the entire day if I have to get up early, and that's the case with most night owls.
>
> **"You Have Fewer Decisions to Make."** She says that working during the early morning hours offers the bonus that it's before regular business hours. Well here's a heads-up: The same is true at night. Morning person or night owl, we all get the same 24 hours every day.
>
> **"You Can Stop Fighting Distractions."** I don't have any distractions at night when all the morning larks are asleep because they can't go the distance.
>
> **"You Can Take Advantage of the Calm."** Night is far calmer than morning. If I have to get up early I hear cars, trucks, dogs barking, and all sorts of distractions. Late at night there's none of that. It's pure quietness and productivity bliss. I'm sorry, Ms. Vozza, but you're spewing nonsense and fueling society's bias against night owls.

It's astonishing to me that such prestigious publications would publish "facts" that are entirely based on one person's bias and are not backed whatsoever by research.

The Problem with Studies Favoring Morning Larks

What this all boils down to is an endless parade of research studies that conclude that morning people perform better at work and school.

As you now know, that's because these studies don't account for the fact that morning people do better at work and school *because* those things start in the morning! Night owls, on the other hand, are left to fend for themselves.

Morning Madness

You'll find hundreds of articles and studies concluding that morning people are more successful in their careers and in their education; however, they do not use proper statistical analysis models to account for the fact that work and school are, by default, favorable to early risers. Night owls are completely ignored and our sleep tendencies are not accounted for.

When you come across these flawed studies, always remember that they're measuring the performance of individuals *in the morning*. If they were to do studies measuring performance in the evening and night hours, early risers would be left in the dust.

5

Fighting Your Internal Clock Is Harmful to Your Health

Getting Up Too Early Can Actually Give You Diabetes

Yes, you read that correctly: Early rising, for those to whom it is unnatural, can literally give you diabetes. Could this be why we have an explosive epidemic of diabetes in America right now? All because of arrogant people who say things like, "Remember, we're conscientious"—but not when it comes to night owls' health, evidently. Oh, and did I mention it can cause heart disease, too?

In any case, medical researchers have uncovered a problem that night owls face. They call it social jetlag.

It's the result of, you guessed it, night owls being forced to conform to a morning-centric society. And it's downright harmful for your health. This is why it's so important to educate employers not only on the loss of productivity caused by forcing night owls to work in the mornings, but also the liability they may face down the road for the resultant health problems.

A study published in the *Journal of Clinical Endocrinology & Metabolism* (I told you I love reading medical studies), entitled "Social Jetlag, Chronotype, and Cardiometabolic Risk," shows exactly how much we night owls put our health at risk when we're forced to get up early for work or school.

To quote the study, "Individuals differ in circadian phase preference, known as chronotype, but may be constrained by modern work obligations to specific sleep schedules. Individuals experience social jetlag (SJL) due to a habitual discrepancy between their endogenous circadian rhythm and actual sleep times imposed by social obligations."

In plain English, the sleep times imposed by society cause social jetlag in those of us with a night owl chronotype. Or to put it more simply, we're chronically fatigued thanks to societal norms and the belief in the morning myth.

I'll skip the medical lingo and give you the brief version of the study's conclusion:

Our findings suggest that a misalignment of sleep timing is associated with metabolic risk factors that predispose to diabetes and atherosclerotic cardiovascular disease.

I hope you read that correctly, because it didn't say we *may* be at risk for diabetes and heart disease. It says that being forced to conform to a morning schedule *predisposes* us to diabetes and heart disease.

How's that for hijinks?

This is all the result of the myth of "early to bed and early to rise…" along with the demands of early riser employers who force their employees to work on their schedule, even though they're putting their employees' health at risk, or at least the health of the night owls, anyway. Those who fall somewhere in between early risers and night owls may also be exposed to some degree of risk.

Here are some more tidbits from that study, before moving on to others:

Short sleep and poor subjective sleep quality elevate the risk for insulin resistance, the metabolic syndrome, obesity, type 2 diabetes, and incident cardiovascular disease…

Physiological processes such as glucose metabolism, core body temperature, and blood pressure (BP) have an intrinsic circadian rhythm that, when disrupted, may contribute to risk for cardiovascular disease. Relative to normal daytime workers, shift workers, who often experience chronic circadian misalignment, are more likely to develop the metabolic syndrome, type 2 diabetes, and coronary heart disease, with relative risk increasing as a function of years spent in shift work. In an experimental study, healthy adults asked to eat and sleep 12 hours out of phase from their regular schedules exhibited vascular and endocrine abnormalities, such as increased arterial pressure, a reversed daily cortisol rhythm, and postprandial glucose levels in the range of a prediabetic state. And in the general population, people are influenced by environmental cues such as *work schedules that may enforce less extreme yet habitual misalignment between their intrinsic circadian clock and actual sleep-wake times, again with a potential impact on cardiometabolic risk.* (Emphasis mine.)

In plain English, if your natural sleep cycle is being constantly disrupted by your work demands, then you'd better have great health insurance and a big fat HSA/FSA account for medical bills down the road. If this isn't motivation to start a business and get out of a job that makes you show up early, I don't know what is.

Continuing on, and even more relevant to us, "A second form of circadian disruption, termed 'social jetlag' (SJL), describes the chronic jetlag-like phenomenon occasioned by modern work schedules and reflects misalignment between an individual's endogenous circadian clock and actual sleep times. More specifically, individuals 'travel back and forth' between 'time zones' on workdays (socially imposed schedules) and free (i.e., nonwork) days. SJL has been linked to measures of adiposity, heart rate, and higher cortisol levels in healthy individuals and to higher glycated hemoglobin levels in patients with type 2 diabetes."

(Translations: "Adiposity" is a fancy medical term for obesity, "cortisol" is the body's stress hormone, which the adrenal glands pump out in response to stressful situations such as waking up too early, "hemoglobin" is the part of red blood cells that deliver iron where needed in the body, and "glycated hemoglobin" is a form of hemoglobin that is used to measure average blood glucose concentration, or, in other words, to what degree, if any, of a diabetic or prediabetic state you may be in.)

It's important to note that this is a *scientific* study, not merely wandering around a campus with a clipboard asking random people questions. It used multiple regression analyses, or in other words, that complicated math that Dr. Lott uses and is way over my head! But that's why the study has credibility and proves that it's accurate.

In addition, the study accounted for health behaviors such as smoking, alcohol intake and how much, diet, and so on; in other words, all room for error was removed from the study.

Rotating Shift Work Exacerbates Health Risks

In a study in the *American Journal of Preventive Medicine*, entitled "Total and Cause-Specific Mortality of U.S. Nurses Working Rotating Night Shifts," the news gets even worse.

Keep in mind that this study includes all chronotypes, and includes morning people who are forced to work night shifts. (Ha, take that, morning people! Now you know what it's like!)

I'm including it since it does apply to us; it's relevant to anyone forced to work on a schedule that conflicts with their natural-born circadian rhythms.

Background: "Rotating night shift work imposes circadian strain and is linked to the risk of several chronic diseases."

I'll spare you the medical lingo this time. The study concludes that those who are forced to work rotating night shifts, defined as greater than three nights per month—which is nothing compared with having to do it five days a week or more for decades, as night owls do—are at significantly elevated risk of elevated heart rate (tachycardia), all-cause mortality (!), cardiovascular death, and lung cancer.

Now I finally understand why only half of lung cancer victims are smokers, since that never made any sense to me; perhaps it's society's insistence on forcing people out of bed at the crack of dawn that's killing them. And this study shows that being forced to work on a schedule that doesn't match up to yours will indeed significantly increase risk of lung cancer.

PubMed, the U.S. National Library of Medicine's website, states that about 15–20% of employees in Europe and the United States are engaged in night shift work. Considering the fact that anywhere between 30–50% of the population are natural-born night owls, their numbers fail to account for the risk that night owls are exposed to when they experience social jetlag, thanks to getting up too early.

They Call Us Narcissists and Psychopaths

"Creatures of the night: Chronotypes and the Dark Triad traits," published in the medical journal *Personality and Individual Differences*, Volume 55, Issue 5 (September 2013), goes so far as to claim that night owls are evil!

The study claims a link between those who stay up late and what psychologists call the "Dark Triad" of personality traits: narcissism, psychopathy, and Machiavellianism.

To quote the lead researcher, Peter K. Johnson of the University of Western Sydney, "We propose that in order to best enact a 'cheater strategy,' those high on the Dark Triad traits should have cognitive performance and, thus, have a night-time chronotype. Such a disposition will take advantage of the low light, the limited monitoring, and the lessened cognitive processing of morning-type people."

Wow. So now we're narcissists, psychopaths, and Machiavellians. You know, the kind of people who commit mass shootings, or who are brutal, totalitarian dictators. Unbelievable! If ever there was an extreme bias against night owls, this is it. To his credit, Mr. Johnson did mention that morning-type people have lessened cognitive processing at night. At least he's right about that.

As usual with these biased studies, it cites no statistical analysis model, which alone makes the study not even worth the paper it's printed on, and shows that it was likely undertaken with ill intent.

Taking it a step further, one can turn the conclusion around on its head, and claim that early risers must be part of the "Dark Triad" since they happen to get up when there's low light, limited monitoring, and when night-type people have lessened cognitive processing. See, the guy discredited himself with his own study!

It's Not Just Diabetes and Heart Disease, It's Stroke, Too

On top of everything else, being forced to rise early against our natural tendencies also carries the risk of stroke.

Express in the UK reported on a study done by scientists in Melbourne, Australia, who also found that rising before sunrise causes social jetlag, a topic we discuss earlier.

A big part of the problem is that our bodies produce melatonin—the sleep hormone—when it's dark, and suppress it when it's light out. That's a primary reason why it's so hard to wake up before it's fully light outside, which typically takes about 30 minutes after sunrise to occur.

As to the health risks, it all boils down to the stress hormone, cortisol. When your body decides that it's time to wake up naturally, it suppresses melatonin and your adrenal glands dump a significant amount of cortisol into your bloodstream, which is what wakes you up.

However, when you're forced to sleep off your natural schedule, there's an imbalance between melatonin and cortisol. In response to the presence of melatonin after rising, cortisol levels skyrocket, and chronically high cortisol levels, along with the imbalance with melatonin, are linked to an increased risk of strokes, heart disease, diabetes, and depression. Furthermore, as you're about to learn in my personal story of attempting to become an early riser, the chronically high levels of cortisol that your adrenal glands produce can also lead to adrenal exhaustion, a state where you're so physically and mentally exhausted that you can't just "push through it." It's not like trying to drive a car on fumes; it's like trying to drive a car off the assembly line that's never had a drop of fuel in it.

My Personal Metabolic Morning Disaster

The primary reason I started a business at 30 years old, or I should say started the first business that succeeded, wasn't the money or the cars or the women or anything like that.

It was simply so I could have a steady income without getting out of bed at an insane hour. I wasn't even after money. I just needed the freedom to be who I am, a night owl, and thankfully I achieved that and was able to quit my last job ever in 2003.

Prior to that, I was stuck getting up for a job, which, even though I liked it, was taxing my body physically and myself mentally. It was the forced early rising that led to my vicious cycle of boatloads of alcohol at night to get to sleep in time to wake up early and then a boatload of coffee the next day to fight through. I'd even turned to a mixture of both caffeine and ephedrine at times, which is downright dangerous in terms of heart health.

Even my coworkers made fun of how much coffee I drank. Since I've never liked Starbucks (with all due apologies to those who do), I stopped at a local gourmet coffee shop called "Jitters" every day, along with a few additional stops throughout the day. If my schedule of appointments didn't bring me past a Jitters location, I'd settle for Starbucks—as long as I had my caffeine fix I could get my work done.

I remember one year, for my birthday, everyone in the office signed a card and one of the guys even drew a big coffee mug with the name "Jitters" on it ... that's how bad my habit was!

Fast-forward to four years ago and the event that made me choose to become an advocate for night owls.

Someone told me about a mastermind group I should join. At the time I was working on getting marketing automation set up in my sales training business, and one of the group's leaders was an expert in that, so I decided to join.

I cannot remember if it was at one of the in-person weekend intensive roundtables that I first received this "advice," or if it was on a call, but either way, several members had read a book that promised the key to massive productivity and success, and here it is: Get up at four or five o'clock in the morning, then do a "ritual."

First of all, getting up at four or five o'clock, unless your body awakens naturally, is insane and unhealthy. Second, when I hear the word "ritual" my mind immediately goes to cults. I have routines, like my gym routines that I do, but ritual? No thanks.

Anyway, after enough convincing, I gave it a try.

Getting up that early was brutal. My wife was first asking me why I was doing it, and then became amazed that I was able to stick with it.

But not for long.

Even though I'd already given up alcohol, which provided surprisingly little benefit in comparison with quitting caffeine, I was still "on the bean," as I've heard some coffee drinkers put it, and I was downing record amounts.

At one point I was drinking six cups a day, and by cups I don't mean the standard eight-ounce measure, I mean big coffee-shop cups, enough to cause the medical disorder known as caffeinism. As part of caffeinism I developed the characteristic anxiety, jitters, and insomnia that are hallmark symptoms of the disorder.

After doing this long enough—and I can't remember how long I did it because that level of fatigue and sleep phase disturbance seriously impairs memory—I became completely exhausted. I'm talking totally wiped out, as if I were wandering through my days like I was under sedation for a medical procedure. It was that bad.

No one else could understand what it was like. It even caused marital problems when I had to continually cancel on events I had planned on attending with my wife, particularly school events such as their big annual auction gala. She would tell me to just push through, which is common sense, but at that level of extreme exhaustion there's nothing to push with. It's like that proverbial car that's never had a drop of fuel in it.

After consulting with my doctor, he sent me home with a diurnal adrenal saliva test kit. (You can find them on Amazon if you'd like to do one yourself—I prefer the ZRT brand.)

The results were shocking: My adrenal glands were barely functioning at all. The cortisol levels throughout the day were at the very bottom of the chart, save for the "second wind" in the late evening that we night owls are accustomed to, and even that was reduced to a small blip. I was diagnosed with adrenal exhaustion and sent to see a nutritionist to set me up on an adrenal adaptogen diet. It worked, but it took the better part of a year to recover. What's even worse is that the lab results, when analyzed alongside the long questionnaire that must be completed, flagged me as having the metabolic syndrome and a potential prediabetic state. Sound familiar?

During that recovery time I had little ability to do anything and my business began to trend downward. It began slowly at first but quickly accelerated to the point where we nearly lost our house, I had to get rid of the six-figure cars I'd been used to driving for over a decade, and many other sacrifices along the way. Not to mention medical expenses.

All of this because of one person's *opinion*—with *zero* science behind it—that getting up at four or five o'clock will make you wildly successful. It's all just more of the endless fallout from the myth of "early to bed and early to rise ..." from a man who didn't even practice what he preached.

The irony in all of this is that everyone I know who is following that program was already getting up by six o'clock in the morning, so it's not a major feat to push that time back one hour. Even still, they're like zombies by early afternoon. Meanwhile it's early afternoon as I write this and I'm wide awake and fully alert!

No, getting up that early didn't make me wildly successful. It made me gravely ill and I nearly went broke. My kids still say, "Daddy just sleeps all the time." No, I don't anymore, but that horrible ordeal lasted so long that I can see why they'd think that. The author of that book is damn lucky I didn't sue him.

Meanwhile, people I know who still buy into that nonsense and are still following the book's plan are useless by afternoon. I remember being on a call with someone I was paying $2,500 a month for services related to my marketing automation and he'd literally be passing out at his desk by 3:00 p.m., if not earlier. The same is true for everyone else I know following the "early to bed and early to rise" plan, regardless of what you call it.

As you'll soon learn, even natural early risers can't go the distance. Most of them are fading by early to mid-afternoon, hence the office coffee machine that's perpetually on, not to mention the popularity of Keurig machines and the explosion not only of Starbucks but more specifically of independent coffee shops everywhere. Those morning people are making them rich, along with night owls forced to abide by their schedules.

Thankfully, a short time after six months had passed with me back on my natural sleep schedule and with minimal caffeine, my cortisol levels were back to normal, and I was no longer even close to being flagged as metabolic syndrome and potential pre-diabetes.

Getting my natural sleep schedule back also gave me back my health!

Even after all that, I was frequently tempted to make an attempt at early rising again, but closer to something like 7:00 a.m., not 4 or 5 a.m. I like seeing my wife and kids before they all leave, but after about a week each time, I realize that I'm harming myself—and eventually them, for financial reasons—and wisely return to my natural schedule.

Why am I frequently tempted to try to get up earlier? Simple: The brainwashing is so pervasive that even the author of this book, *The Morning Myth*, sometimes starts to wonder if it's true.

If I can fall for that absurdity, it's no wonder that most of society believes it, too, and suffers as a result.

Morning Madness

Medical science has proven that deviating from your normal sleep schedule puts you at risk for heart disease, stroke, cancer, adrenal failure, and many more health problems. Meanwhile, advocates of early rising go so far as to call us "evil" and classify us with the worst of human society. It's no wonder, then, that so many fall for the morning myth.

CHAPTER

6

Your Circadian Rhythm—
and Why You Can't
Change It

The Internal Clock You're
Born With Is the One
You're Stuck With

B ooks, books, books.
    Aside from the infamous one that I referred to in the previous chapter, I can't even count how many books I've read on success, self-improvement, and the biographies and autobiographies of countless successful people.

Meanwhile, I also can't remember exactly how many of them preached the wonders, merits, and even morality of getting up at extreme hours.

It was very common to read about how they were all up at 5:00 a.m. each day! That makes me wonder how many of them were actually telling the truth, considering the fact that Ben Franklin was a late riser in spite of his famous advice, and even I've told little white lies about what time I get up to avoid the night owl stigma and the label of "lazy" and so on.

Come to think of it, most of them got up at 5:00 a.m. on their fathers' orders. No wonder they're preaching that nonsense, when the brainwashing was forced upon them at such a young age, an age when kids need many more hours than adults to sleep and maintain healthy growth and development. It really makes one wonder how much more they might have achieved had they been allowed to sleep on a child's normal schedule instead of being forced out of bed before dawn like a Marine recruit at boot camp.

Hours a Day—but Not for You

Your circadian rhythm determines when you naturally fall asleep and when you naturally awaken. Here is the typical human circadian rhythm beginning in the evening; keep in mind that everyone is different, which we'll get to shortly (and notice that in a "typical" circadian rhythm, natural awakening occurs around 7:30 a.m.):

6:30 p.m.: Highest blood pressure
7:00 p.m.: Highest body temperature
9:00 p.m.: Melatonin secretion starts
10:30 p.m.: Bowel movements suppressed
2:00 a.m.: Deepest sleep (again, this is "typical," and not specific to night owls)

4:30 a.m.: Lowest body temperature (this is when I frequently wake up briefly to turn off the ceiling fan)

6:45 a.m.: Blood pressure rapidly increases

7:30 a.m.: Melatonin secretion stops (natural waking time)

8:30 a.m.: Bowel movement likely (too much info, I know)

9:00 a.m.: Highest testosterone levels in men

10:00 a.m.: High alertness

2:30 p.m.: Best coordination

3:30 p.m.: Fastest reaction time

5:00 p.m.: Greatest cardiovascular efficiency and muscle strength (meaning hit the gym! Or at 9:00 a.m. if you're a man, when that big testosterone rush hits.)

And there you have it. This is what your body does around the clock, and it's all governed by our inborn circadian rhythms. As a general rule, women tend to have shorter rhythms and get up earlier, but again, that's just, well, "typical." Everyone is different.

What I find most interesting about this example is something I've stated earlier, that it takes two full hours to become fully alert and achieve peak cognitive function. That's why I broke the habit of getting up and immediately grabbing my laptop and getting some work done. (Also, the medical hypnotherapist I was seeing for the anxiety that that stupid book caused strongly advised me to stop doing that.)

Congratulations! You've Won 25 Hours a Day!

Well, maybe not congratulations. It's more like a problem, but only because society says it is. Personally, I consider it an asset.

Many call it a "disorder" rather than recognizing it for what it is—the fact that everyone's sleep cycle is different. Just like we're all unique in such things as the color of our hair, eyes, skin, height, weight, voice, nationality, and so on, we're all born with a unique circadian rhythm.

It's this habit of calling a later, or actually, a *longer* circadian rhythm, a "disorder" that causes much of the stigma about night owls being lazy and slothful and everything else they can think of. Just as former president George W. Bush is fighting to remove the word "disorder" from PTSD, or post-traumatic stress disorder, our modern society must start recognizing that a different sleep cycle in others is no different than someone having different color hair or a different shoe size than one's self.

There's absolutely no "disorder" in having a sleep cycle that differs from the average person. After all, no one is calling early risers out as having a "disorder" for being up at five o'clock. Instead, they're celebrated, while we're stigmatized and labeled.

Here's where it gets interesting: While there are a fixed 24 hours in a day, human circadian rhythms vary wildly from exactly 24 hours in extreme early risers, to 25 hours in those with what's known as delayed sleep phase disorder (DSPD), or those who typically can't fall asleep until five or six in the morning.

So when Tim Cook, CEO of Apple, blasts out one of his obnoxious tweets bragging about how he was up at 4:30 a.m. (yet again), or some self-righteous morning person who thinks they're better than you brags about getting up at 5:00 a.m., what they're really subcommunicating to you is, "I have a 24-hour circadian rhythm or close to it. Why don't you?"

As with racism, people are afraid and even hateful of those who differ from themselves, and that's where the discrimination against night owls comes from. There's no logic or reason to it, just prejudice, and an "I'm better than you" attitude, just because they got up at an hour when most people are still in bed.

On the other end of the scale, I've already mentioned DSPD, where someone has a circadian rhythm that is at or near 25 hours. This is indeed problematic since those with DSPD can experience extreme difficulty coping in modern society and holding on to good jobs. On the other hand, they may be prime candidates for overnight shift jobs during those hours when morning people cannot possibly stay awake. Better yet, they can be like Mark Cuban, who stayed up all night in his twenties learning coding, and now he's a billionaire. That's not a bad option either!

Your inborn circadian rhythm is called your chronotype, and your chronotype is just as fixed as all of your other physical characteristics. You cannot change it. Or, I should say, you can temporarily, but it will soon catch up with you and you'll find yourself back on your natural schedule. There is a method that physicians use to "treat" those with DSPD, but the effects do not endure long-term.

Having said that, you can change your wake time by an hour, maybe two hours if you're lucky, just as those friends I've mentioned who used to get up at six o'clock and now get up at five o'clock have done.

As a general rule, morning people have a rhythm closer to 24 hours, with somewhere around 24.3 considered "intermediate," or those who are neither early risers nor night owls. Night owl rhythms can run as long as 24.5–24.7 hours. Anything beyond that, up to 25 hours, falls under DSPD.

(Note: In doing my research for this book, I'm increasingly—and sadly—seeing the term "delayed sleep phase disorder" being thrown around to describe anyone who isn't up at the crack of dawn, even though it affects only 0.2% of the population. It's yet another example of the prejudice and labels night owls must suffer.)

You Can't Change Your Inborn Chronotype— You Can Only Adapt

Whether you're an early riser, a night owl, or one of those "normal" people in between, the reality is that your natural chronotype is inborn, it's genetic, and attempting to change it will be frustrating, fruitless, and harmful to your physical health and well-being.

Bear with me here while I get all scientific on you:

The suprachiasmatic nucleus (let's just stick with SCN) is a tiny region within the brain, located in the hypothalamus, that is responsible for regulating your circadian rhythm and is hard-wired to follow the chronotype that is yours.

Normally, your body regulates itself through natural daylight. When outdoor-intensity light is sensed by the human body, melatonin production is abruptly ceased and cortisol comes rushing out of the adrenal glands, into the bloodstream and brain, to wake you up.

However, with night owls, or anyone with more than 24.3 hours to their chronotype, it's not exactly that simple.

(By the way, if you're wondering how "normal" people can live in a 24-hour world when they get 24.3 hours, it's bright morning light that somehow "rolls back" that 0.3 of an hour and resets them back to 24 hours.)

While the SCN is normally the body's master clock regulator, just like those 555 clock chips for those who were also electronic geeks as kids (though they're still in use now), a large genetic component comes into play, and twin and heredity studies have shown a strong link between chronotype and genes, explaining why my siblings are also night owls.

Just like the SCN is the body's clock and the 555 chip is the most common electronics clock, your body has clock genes that can regulate the expression of upwards of 20% of all of the other genes in every cell.

These genes feed back into the master clock—the SCN—and influence its time. Researchers have found that even small variations in those genes lead to earlier or later than average chronotypes as a result. The more of these genes in one's body, the harder the SCN must work to attempt to regulate the circadian rhythm, and frequently it simply cannot fully adjust.

To further complicate matters, it's been found that night owls, or anyone in general who tends toward the evening hours over morning, may be unusually sensitive to light exposure at night. That's why you hear all that advice about "no blue light" before bedtime, and they're right, especially for us night owls. Those with DSPD are even advised to keep the blinds closed and wear dark sunglasses after 3:00 p.m. in order to have any hope of falling asleep at night.

As for me personally, I wear blue-blocking glasses (no magnification) for television and any other activities in the evening and night that might interfere with sleep. I use the "night shift" feature on my computers, iPad, and iPhone, along with the f.lux app, and combine all of that with the blue-blocker glasses; they're cheap on Amazon. You can also get reading glasses with the yellow blue-blocking tint, which I'm starting to need at my age, particularly when I'm very tired. Speaking of Amazon, where you can find anything that exists, there are even blue-blocking protective screen covers for phones, laptops, and tablets that are another option.

The reason for blocking blue light is that it suppresses melatonin production; because the sky is blue and daylight is toward the blue end of the color temperature scale, the brain misinterprets blue screen light as daylight, which in turn unnaturally delays bedtime.

By the way, once chronotype is set by your natural-born clock, your genes, and the time of day your body becomes accustomed to sensing morning daylight, it's damn near written in stone. According to Leon Lack, a circadian rhythm researcher at Flinders University in Australia, "Our feeling at this point is that these are probably unchangeable characteristics."

The one exception is that people tend to awaken earlier as they age; however, this isn't due to the popular myth that less sleep is needed as the years accumulate. The reality is that the body's melatonin production drops with age and reaches a point where it's not producing enough. This is why it's so common to hear older people complain about waking up too early, or of insomnia.

What happened is that evolution lags by about 100,000 years. So we're living in bodies that are made for ancient times when we went to sleep after sundown and arose shortly after sunrise, and that, more important, aren't fully developed to live as long as we are now thanks to advances in medical technology.

The end result is that modern humans find themselves unable to sleep as much with age. While many believe that older age means a reduced sleep requirement, what's really happening is a melatonin deficiency that can be remedied with a safe, low dose of melatonin 1–2 hours before planned bedtime.

Medical Treatments for Delayed Sleep Phase Disorder

Doctors have come up with some ways to attempt to treat DSPD—I say "attempt" because the result is never permanent. However, they do help some with DSPD to function semi-normally in a morning-centric society.

The following are the most common.

Light Therapy (Phototherapy)

This is the practice of either getting out of bed and immediately getting outside into bright sunlight, or, alternatively, using a therapy lamp with a brightness of at least 10,000 lux, or, to put it more simply, enough light to suppress melatonin secretion and send the signal to your body to wake up.

I use one on days when I want to get up early, or have to for some business or school event. Since jumping out of bed early really doesn't work for me, I keep one on my nightstand and use it for 30 minutes while reading something on my Kindle. Nowadays they're available as small LED-powered lamps instead of the big fluorescent monstrosities of only a decade ago, which also makes them portable and inexpensive. (WARNING: Do not begin the use of a therapy lamp without consulting an eye doctor if you have macular degeneration, or even a family history of the same. If you're not sure, ask around your family.)

Darkness Therapy (Light Restriction)

Remember I had mentioned that DSPD patients are advised to wear dark sunglasses past 3:00 p.m., and that I use blue-blocking glasses along with blue-light diminishing features and apps on my various electronic devices? Darkness therapy is the reason why.

Phase Delay Chronotherapy

This therapy is normally only used with severe DSPD patients, and even then, it's falling out of favor due to doubts about its safety and a track record of leading to non-24-hour sleep-wake rhythm disorder, a far more serious and severe disorder.

In phase delay chronotherapy, the patient goes to bed two hours later each night until the desired bedtime is reached (obviously it takes some time off from work or school to accomplish this). Once that bedtime is reached, the patient is then advised to go to bed at that same time every night.

However, the body is always working to achieve homeostasis, which is a fancy way of saying an ideal state. As part of that, it works hard to get back to your natural born chronotype, and patients who undergo this treatment must repeat it anywhere from every few weeks (!) to every few months.

A modified version of this plan is called SDPA: controlled sleep deprivation with phase advance. With this, the person stays awake overnight and all through the next day, then goes to bed 90 minutes earlier than the desired bedtime and maintains that for a week. The process is repeated weekly until the new bedtime "sticks."

There isn't enough research on SDPA to show whether or not it will work in the long run, but if previous methods are any evidence, it won't, and it's potentially unsafe, just as phase delay chronotherapy may be.

Melatonin

A small dose of melatonin about an hour before the desired bedtime *may* induce sleepiness (it doesn't work very well for me personally, hence the "may").

Melatonin doesn't come without its own share of problems, though. While healthy lifestyle websites and blogs tout it as a powerful antioxidant, and it is, it can also cause sleep disturbance, nightmares, daytime sleepiness, and even depression.

If you have had, or if there is any family history of melanoma, the deadly form of skin cancer, then you *must not* take melatonin. If you are in any doubt, please consult your physician.

The U.S. Department of Health and Human Services has found little difference between melatonin and placebo for primary and secondary sleep disorders, so take everything you hear with a grain of salt.

Modafinil (Brand Name: Provigil)

This is a strong stimulant used in the U.S. military, particularly with pilots who must fly very long missions, for whom it is mandatory.

While it does in fact help a sleep-deprived individual get through the day with mental alertness and acuity, it has an extremely long elimination half-life, meaning it has a strong likelihood of interfering with sleep and even causing insomnia.

I personally asked my own doctor about it after hearing that it was a wonder productivity drug and his response was that just like excessive caffeine, it will lead to adrenal exhaustion, which was all I needed to hear. I'll pass.

But Will Treatment Work?

As you can see, there's very little here that's anything remotely scientific, with the exceptions being light and darkness therapy.

Even the medically approved methods of changing one's sleep schedule—phase delay chronotherapy and controlled sleep deprivation with phase advance—are only temporary and must be repeated over and over and over to remain effective (or at least their definition of effective). All these treatments do is put the patient through a hellish roller-coaster ride of sleep deprivation when they should simply be allowed to live and work on the sleep schedules they were born with. It's all just more fallout from the discrimination and brainwashing, fallout that is messing with people's lives and well-being.

Instead of coming up with labels like "delayed sleep phase disorder," and assuming there's something medically wrong with those who go to bed very late and get up late, society should accommodate and not alienate such people.

Can You Really Get Up Earlier—and Live to Tell About It?

As with far too many things in life, the answer is maybe, and closer to probably not.

If you're a mild night owl, say, someone who can go to bed by midnight and get up at seven o'clock, then perhaps you can.

If you're any much more of a night owl than that, sure, you may be able to get up an hour earlier, but you still won't conform to current societal norms, so what's the point? After all, it's only going to harm your health in the long term.

However, if you really would like to have a go at it, or if you're getting up at seven o'clock but need to be up at six o'clock to get to work on time, a combination of light therapy and darkness therapy is probably the safest option, and most likely to work.

For starters, I recommend getting a therapy lamp. As I've said, they're cheap on Amazon, eBay, and other online sellers. You can, of course, get outside into sunlight immediately, but c'mon, we both know that's not going to happen! And, once again, if macular degeneration runs in your family, *do not* use one, at least not without visiting with an ophthalmologist first. If *you* have macular degeneration, forget it.

Follow the directions that come with the lamp; they do differ in brightness and that will determine how far it needs to be from your eyes along with how long you need to use it. Since they're so bright, never look directly into the light, but rather simply have it within your field of vision. For me, I sit up in bed and keep it slightly off to the side of my Kindle (or book) so my eyes are exposed without directly looking at it.

The key to light therapy is to activate the light at your desired waking time; however, don't jump an hour back in one fell swoop. The most you can realistically work with is 10–15 minutes earlier, every two to three days. Any faster than that and you'll crash. Slower is better, but we humans are impatient. And remember this may not work at all; it's simply a suggestion. Continue to do so until you reach your desired waking time, then continue the light therapy; remember, you're going against your inborn chronotype here, so while you can probably knock back your wake time by 10 or 15 minutes, it's still a long-term change.

Therapy light bonus: They're great for jetlag! And now that they're small and lightweight, you can easily pack one when you travel.

With darkness therapy, as with light therapy, the goal is to get to bed 10–15 minutes earlier, every few days. Now that most of the year is Daylight Saving Time in the United States, what I do is to close the blackout curtains in our house by 7:00 p.m. and then use the blue-blocking glasses with any electronics including television, computers, phones, and everything in between.

As I've mentioned, I've tried melatonin, but it didn't work for me. If you do try it, you'll probably need to go to a specialty health food store with a large vitamin/supplement section to find 0.3 mg melatonin tablets. The usual 3 mg and 5 mg dosages found in common over-the-counter melatonin products are extremely excessive and may leave you feeling sluggish and groggy the next day, which entirely defeats the purpose. And, again, if you have any family history of melanoma whatsoever, *do not* use melatonin at *any* dosage.

Be forewarned though: Unless you want to keep doing all this forever, your sleep cycle is your sleep cycle and it's going to revert back to baseline sooner or later, and probably sooner.

Morning Madness

You were born with your natural, built-in clock. Accept it. Live with it. Use it to thrive. Most important of all, don't fight it, and if you must do so for work or other reasons, be aware that any changes to your sleep schedule that you make are likely only temporary. The real solution is flexible working hours, and if your current employer won't give them to you, there are better ones who will.

7

Night Owls Are More Successful

The Early Birds Just Don't Make As Much Money

It all comes down to one thing: Early risers who get up at the crack of dawn tire far earlier than their night owl counterparts and, overall, experience fewer productive hours each day.

In other words, night owls make more money and are generally more successful in life because they have more usable, productive working hours available, despite the common myth that getting up super early is the only way to accomplish this and to "make more time," as idiots who cannot do basic math and understand that we all get the same 24 hours every day will tell you.

There's no way to "make more time." All you can do is make the most of the time you have. And that amount of time is the same for all of us, unlike our biological chronotypes, which can vary wildly from anywhere from 24 hours for extreme early risers and 25 hours for extreme night owls, or those with delayed sleep phase disorder.

The Night Owl Experience That Set Me Free

To demonstrate, let me tell you a story.

Back in September of 2001, I was on top of the world saleswise and was beyond 100% of my monthly number by the 10th of the month.

Then September 11, 2001 happened.

What I remember most about that day—and I remember it vividly, as most people do—was getting up for work on Phoenix time, and since Arizona does not practice Daylight Saving Time, the time difference between Phoenix and "back home" in New Jersey was three hours.

As always, I checked my phone for anything important and saw two missed calls and voicemails, one from my mom and one from my dad. (They're divorced and live separately.)

I naturally panicked, thinking a grandparent or other relative had passed away. I checked the voicemails fearing the worst. What I heard from my dad was a message letting me know that my sister was okay, since her dorm at New York University was very close to the World Trade Center, and in fact she was evacuated and couldn't return for quite a while after.

My mom, on the other hand, was looking to me for guidance, asking, "What's happening?" and "Are we going to be okay?"

I watched the footage on the television news, almost in tears. You see, as a kid growing up in New Jersey just outside NYC, one of my favorite things to do was to go up to the observation deck at the World Trade Center and stare in awe at the views. And the radio antennas, too, since I'm a ham radio geek, but that's another story.

Seeing one of my favorite childhood memories collapse into rubble was heartbreaking.

Driving to work that day all I can remember was how angry I felt, and how violated we all seemed to be with an act of war occurring in our own homeland.

But I digress. The point of this story is that after exceeding my monthly number by the 10th of September 2001, for the rest of the month my sales totaled exactly $0.

And October. And November. Then came the holiday season and the usual, time-worn excuse of, "We'll be ready sometime after the first of the year."

Needless to say, I was going broke fast. Granted, I'd made a lot of money but being a single twentysomething, I was driving a luxury car and living the life and going out five nights a week partying. Now don't get me wrong; I highly recommend that everyone enjoy that lifestyle at some point in their lives! Just be prepared for the financial fallout after the fact.

My employer went broke thanks to the sudden halt in sales revenue. Commissions were cut back to nothing, so I left that sales position and instead of just getting another job, I became an independent agent for every telecom provider in Phoenix. That way, I totally eliminated competition, and instead presented the best solutions from every provider. That way I won every sale and no one else was even invited to compete.

The year 2002 was slow and rough. It was a challenge to make a good living with the deep recession 9/11 had caused. Finally, I decided that enough was enough and I needed to find a way out.

I wanted to stop trading my time for money and start experiencing financial freedom.

To motivate myself, I went to a Mercedes-Benz dealer and sat in a new S500 sedan. I became fixated on it. I burned the image of that car's interior into my mind and every time I drove my lesser luxury car, I saw myself in that S-Class Mercedes.

Then the idea came: It hit me that I'd made my money and achieved such high levels of sales success simply because I had stopped cold calling—a massive time drain for anyone in sales— and instead put into place what I called "self-marketing." And yes, I'm the guy who first coined that term.

By self-marketing, I had leads coming in on autopilot. It's why I was bringing in 50% of the entire company's sales revenue, until that company collapsed post-9/11. When it occurred to me that so many of my fellow sales professionals were constantly asking me to teach them my lead-generation systems, I realized I had a marketable amount of knowledge.

With that in mind, I went to Trader Joe's on a Friday afternoon and literally loaded the trunk of my big Lincoln Town Car with all kinds of frozen, microwave stuff that was delicious yet I'm certain it was horrible for me! Nevertheless, it was enough to get me through the weekend to come.

I sat down on that Friday evening and began writing. I went straight through Friday night, all day Saturday, and once the e-book was completed I recorded two CDs, which took me overnight Saturday into Sunday. By then the product was completed and I finally got some sleep!

The next day, I put up a website, paid my five dollars to open a Google AdWords account, and had my first $67 sale only 30 minutes later. The rest, as they say, is history. Only nine months later I was writing a check for that Mercedes-Benz S500, which was the first of four consecutive S-Classes in a row, all brand-new. I'd also found financial freedom, did not have a job since then in 2003, and of course it came full-circle and made me a *New York Times* best-seller.

Now compare this with an early riser, the types who get up at five and can't stop telling everyone how great they are as a result. You know, the kinds who just want to get in your face when they see your morning grogginess and be that annoying, hyper morning person everyone wants to just throw down and be done with.

Personal experience has proven to me that early risers literally cannot work past three o'clock in the afternoon. If you can manage to catch one still working—not just sitting in the office, mind you, but actually being productive—it'll be through endless yawns and baggy eyes.

That's the problem with early risers: They simply cannot go the distance and night owls obliterate them in the long run.

(And seriously—do these people even care about their appearance? Can they not see how U.S. presidents age about 20 years in only eight, thanks to all the early mornings and sleep deprivation? It's no wonder anti-aging skin care is such a massively huge industry!)

Remember that god-awful book I followed, that threw my adrenal and endocrine health into a tailspin and cost me a small fortune in lost production as a result? Everyone I know who is on that program calls it quits by three every afternoon.

3:00 p.m. That's when kids get out of school, not when adults give up the ghost for the day. I even disengaged from a business coach I was working with, specifically because he was following that dumbass book, and when it was time for me to get on the phone with him, I had to listen to "yawn, yawn, yawn" just as I was hitting my peak cognitive function for the day.

Worse yet, the quality of their work suffers if they try to "push through," and there's no one quite like a morning person to try to shove the "just push through" nonsense down your throat. Or at least they do this in the mornings; in the afternoon when we're kicking their asses, they tend to shut up because they know they've been defeated.

Interestingly, when I was experiencing adrenal exhaustion and literally had no gas in the tank, it was morning people—and only morning people—who kept trying to shove the "just push through" crap down my throat, as if they were mocking me. (Which they were. But now it's our turn.)

Also on that note, as I write this book I can tell you I don't even bother starting until about 1–2 p.m. in the afternoon. If I try earlier, or get up early to write, it's a nonstarter. I'll sit here staring at the computer screen like a drooling idiot, like the morning larks are doing by mid-afternoon each day. That's when I go and get my Fox News fix, because I know any work product too early in the day will be garbage.

The Proof Is in the Pudding (or, in This Case, the Research)

In an article in *foundr*, Amy Rigby wrote this short paragraph that I couldn't agree with more:

One day I was standing in the grocery store checkout line when the bagger covered her mouth to stifle a yawn. The shopper in front of me quipped, "If you're going to fly with the night owls, you can't soar with the eagles in the morning."

How true that is! The early birds literally cannot fly with us!

In a study published in the *BMJ* (formerly the *British Medical Journal*), research fellow Catharine Gale and clinical scientist

Christopher Martyn conducted research to, literally, test Benjamin Franklin's maxim "early to bed and early to rise makes a man healthy, wealthy, and wise."

The study included 1,229 men and women; in other words, it used a large sample size, which in turn leads to improved accuracy. The main outcome measures were income, access to a car, standard of accommodation, performance on a test of cognitive function, state of health, and mortality during 23 years of follow-up.

And here are the results: 356 people (29%) were defined as larks (to bed before 11 p.m. and up before 8 a.m.) and 318 (26%) were defined as owls (to bed at or after 11 p.m. and up at or after 8 a.m.). There was no indication that larks were richer than those with other sleeping patterns. On the contrary, owls had the largest mean income and were more likely to have access to a car. There was also no evidence that larks were superior to those with other sleeping patterns with regard to their cognitive performance or their state of health. Both larks and owls had a slightly reduced risk of death compared with the rest of the study sample, but this was accounted for by the fact that they spent less time in bed at night. In the study sample as a whole, longer periods of time in bed were associated with increased mortality. After adjustment for age, sex, the presence of illness, and other risk factors, people who spent 12 or more hours in bed had a relative risk of death of 1.7 (1.2 to 2.5) compared with those who were in bed for 9 hours. The lowest risk occurred in people who spent 8 hours in bed (adjusted relative risk 0.8; 0.7 to 1.0).

Conclusion: These findings do not support Franklin's claim. A "late to bed and late to rise" lifestyle does not seem to lead to socioeconomic, cognitive, or health disadvantage, but a longer time spent in bed may be associated with increased mortality.

Key Messages

Proverbial advice about lifestyle has the authority of tradition
and the merit of brevity, but it is rarely based on systemati-
cally collected evidence.

In a nationally representative cohort of elderly people there
was no indication that those who lived by the maxim
"early to bed and early to rise" were advantaged as re-
gards state of health, material circumstances, or wisdom.

Sleeping for more than eight hours a night was associated with
increased mortality, but it mattered little whether sleep was
taken in the early or late part of the night.

There is no justification for early risers to affect moral superiority.
[Emphasis mine.]

So there you have it, in just one of many studies you're going
to learn about. And I could not agree more with the researchers'
conclusion: "There is no justification for early risers to affect
moral superiority."

So then why do they do it?

There's all kinds of speculation about why a man might
drive a huge lifted pickup truck, or a Lamborghini, or whatever
else. Usually there's a reference to needing to compensate for
something that, umm, isn't quite large enough.

Personally I disagree with that, considering there's no proof
to show that a man who intentionally drives a rundown car must
therefore be extremely well-hung. People only say these things
out of envy, or more specific to us, out of insecurity.

As to morning people, or at least the ones who have an
attitude problem about it and need to announce to the world
just how morally superior they are, I must speculate that there's
something missing from their lives.

Perhaps it's because they earn less than night owls? Maybe they're aware of this fact and feel the need to compensate in other ways.

Or maybe they've noticed that we're just getting warmed up right about the time when they begin to fade fast, aware that their productive hours are coming to a rapid close?

Here's one thing I do know: I have no shame about being a night owl and a late riser. I've taken shit for it my entire life, primarily from people who are *forced* to be up early and *have no choice* in the matter.

In other words, the most likely working hypothesis is that they're envious and insecure about the fact that I don't have to get up at the crack of dawn, while they have an overbearing boss who demands that they do.

Remember when I spent Friday through Sunday creating the product that would bring me financial freedom, and did so almost immediately? Good luck getting a morning person to pull that off. If you had one in your employ and ordered that person to go straight through from Friday through Sunday creating a new product—and this is no exaggeration when you consider what Silicon Valley working hours are like—all you're going to get are excuses about how they need to be in bed by ten so they can get up early and work!

At which point, you, as the employer, would say, "Hey, hang on, that wasn't what I asked of you. I asked—no, ordered—you to get this done in one weekend, sleep or no sleep."

Morning person: "But... but..."

Sorry, early riser, but we don't accept excuses here. To quote the comedian Andrew Dice Clay, "If you can't party with the big boys, *don't show up*."

One thing I know about being an Internet entrepreneur is that virtually all of us are night owls. Oh, and we're part of the crowd that's always posting photos of our awesome cars and vacations and all the other cool shit we have and do—precisely because we can go the distance over and over and over, while the morning larks crash just like a bird into a glass window.

To further quote the study from the *BMJ*:

We found no evidence, however, that following Franklin's advice about going to bed and getting up early was associated with any health, socioeconomic, or cognitive advantage. If anything, owls were wealthier than larks....

What more do you need to know? To further quote the study before moving on:

Folk Wisdom: Although folklore about sleep and sleeping patterns is inconsistent, most sayings, stories, and instances seem to run parallel with Franklin's maxim. Early rising and not sleeping for too long is seen as a recipe for worldly success and even to confer moral superiority. Thomas Edison believed that too much sleep was bad for health and slowed the progress of civilisation. Appropriately enough, he invented the electric lightbulb. Margaret Thatcher, an exemplar of vigour and decisiveness, famously needed little sleep.

And Samuel Johnson cautioned that "nobody who does not rise early will ever do any good," though the force of this advice is rather diminished by his admission that he invariably lay in bed till noon himself. On the other hand, there are proverbial warnings about not burning the candle at both ends and Shakespearian allusions to the restorative powers of sleep. In Henry IV, sleep is described as "nature's soft nurse" and in Macbeth as "chief nourisher in life's feast" and as "knit[ing] up the ravell'd sleave of care."

Our results suggest that, though it may be wise not to spend much more than 8 hours in bed each night, the time of going to bed and getting up matters little. It seems that owls need not worry that their way of life carries adverse consequences. However, *those who cite Franklin's maxim to encourage their children to go to bed early may wish to consider whether their practice is entirely ethical.* [Emphasis mine]

"...is entirely ethical." This study not only disproves the old Ben Franklin maxim of early to bed and early to rise, but even goes so far as to question whether or not it is ethical to encourage one's very own children to follow that advice!

The BBC Speaks Up

As I've mentioned several times thus far, most of the world understands that people will be who they are, whether that be an early riser, a night owl, or somewhere in between. The idea that getting up at four or five in the morning is the "secret" to success is a uniquely American, macho load of bullshit.

So it's no surprise that we must look overseas for accurate research on this topic. Here's an interesting tidbit from the BBC:

Night owls tend to perform better on measures of memory, processing speed and cognitive ability, even when they have to perform those tasks in the morning. Night-time people are also more open to new experiences and seek them out more. They may be more creative (although not always). And contrary to the maxim ("healthy, wealthy and wise"), one study showed that night owls are as healthy and wise as morning types—and a little bit wealthier.

Yep, a little bit wealthier. Not to mention the fact that we're just as healthy and just as wise, and to really add insult to early risers' injury, we perform better in terms of cognitive ability and raw brainpower—even in the mornings!

Is it any real surprise, then, that so much innovation and leaps in technology occur late at night, on that Silicon Valley sleep schedule, when the early risers of the world are fast asleep and we're up burning the midnight oil?

Tim Cook, CEO of Apple, is especially obnoxious about announcing to the world how early he gets up each day. So when I see one of his tweets, with his morally superior "It's great to be up at 3:45 a.m." (seriously dude, get a life!), all I can think is he must be in bed by eight in order to get enough sleep to remain healthy.

Or take former president George W. Bush. When I belonged to a group called the Dallas Business Alliance, which was so good even I was willing to attend every Wednesday at 7:30 a.m., we met in the same building and at the same time that President Bush shows up at his office.

He's up at five each day. Early? Yes! However, the catch is that he can't stay up past 10. If you can remember way back to 2000, he made headlines for leaving the Inaugural balls early so he could hit the sack by 10.

So either way you look at it, they're not squeezing in any extra hours on us, and on top of that, an early riser chronotype leads to fatigue and the dreaded crash earlier in the day than most.

More Science Proving Night Owls Fare Better in Life

A study of approximately 1,000 teenagers conducted by the University of Madrid (notice how they're rarely done in the United States?) found that those who preferred to stay up late exhibited the kind of intelligence associated with better jobs and higher salaries.

To quote the study, "Night owls performed better than early risers at inductive reasoning and demonstrated a greater capacity to think conceptually as well as analytically."

While the study did show that morning larks perform better at school, this was dismissed due to the fact that school starts early in the morning and is therefore biased toward morning larks.

In a study done by the U.S. Air Force (shocker!), it was shown that recruits who are late risers are better at lateral thinking than morning types.

A University of Southampton study found that night owls have higher incomes and higher standards of living overall.

Professor Jim Horne, of Loughborough University, said, "Evening types tend to be the more extrovert creative types, the poets, artists, and inventors, while the morning types are the deducers, as often seen with civil servants and accountants."

He continues, "We have looked at morning and evening types and we found that personalities tended to be different. Evening types were more social, more people-oriented."

Now bear with me here, because I'm about to tie my personal life experience and observations of others into why night owls make more money on the whole.

I happen to have a younger sister, along with a much younger half-brother and half-sister.

As I watched them go through school, the one bit of advice I kept giving was this: "School doesn't matter once you're in the real world. All that matters are social skills. If you can be an outgoing, extroverted, people-oriented person, you will win in this world. That's all there is to success."

Looking back on my own life, the major changes from struggle to success occurred as I got rid of my old introverted self and became an outgoing extrovert, always eager to socialize and meet new people.

And—drumroll, please—that's how business gets done and that's how money is made.

So, while this isn't a controlled research study, if there's one thing I've learned in life, it's that social skills and the ability to be a people person are the true "secrets" to success, and as you now know, night owls possess these skills to an exponentially greater degree than our early riser counterparts, who tend to be introverted and socially awkward as a whole.

Morning Madness

Society still pushes Ben Franklin's maxim to be early to bed and early to rise; however, the facts and the science contradict that maxim. In the real world, night owls make more money, have higher standards of living, more access to cars, more social success... more of everything, really. So remember the British study stating that there is no justification for early risers to affect moral superiority, and tell them to put up or shut up!

CHAPTER

8

Night Owls Are Smarter Than Early Risers

Night Owls Show Overall Higher Intelligence Than Morning People

You now know that night owls make more money and are more successful, so it's only logical to assume that they must be more intelligent.

If you assumed so, you are correct. Studies show that night owls are more intelligent, have higher cognitive ability, are more creative, and much more.

Satoshi Kanazawa, in an article in *Psychology Today* dated May 9, 2010, posits a hypothesis based on observation of certain cultures who rise and go to sleep each day in rhythm with the sun, versus those who stay up past dark and use those hours productively. To quote the article,

> Daily activities begin early in a Yanomamö village, and despite the inevitable last-minute visiting, things are usually quiet in the village by the time it is dark. Among the Maasai in Kenya, the day begins about 6 a.m., when the sun is about to rise, and most evenings are spent quietly chatting with family members indoors. If the moon is full then it is possible to see almost as well as during the day, and people take advantage of the light by staying up late and socializing a great deal. Among the Ache in Paraguay, after cooking and consuming food, evening is often the time of singing and joking. Eventually band members drift off to sleep, with one or two nuclear families around each fire."

He goes on to note that there is no indication in any of the enthographic evidence that any sustained nocturnal activities occur in traditional societies, and that they must have also limited daily activities to daylight, and that nighttime activities are likely evolutionarily novel, and therefore that more intelligent individuals are more likely to be nocturnal.

Looking at modern society to confirm this hypothesis, an analysis of a very large sample of young American children was taken, across a broad number of social and demographic factors.

Conclusion? The numbers show that the most intelligent children grow up to be far more nocturnal as adults than their less intelligent counterparts. More intelligent individuals go to bed later on weeknights regardless of what time they have to get up, and get up later all days when possible.

Children with an average IQ of 75, considered "very dull," went to bed at 11:41 p.m. on weeknights in early adulthood while those who had a childhood IQ of over 125, or "very bright," go to bed as young adults at 12:29 a.m. on average.

Oh, and the sample size in this study consisted of 20,745 subjects. That large a sample virtually guarantees that any coincidental or other outside effect on the numbers will not occur.

More Science to Back Night Owls' Superior Intelligence

In a study published in Elsevier's *Personality and Individual Differences*, Satoshi Kanazawa and Kaja Perina sought to determine where differences in individual values, preferences, and, yes, intelligence come from.

Before getting into this, here's the abstract of their study, summed up nicely:

The origin of values and preferences is an unresolved theoretical problem in social and behavioral sciences. The Savanna–IQ Interaction Hypothesis suggests that more intelligent individuals are more likely to acquire and espouse evolutionarily novel values and preferences than less intelligent individuals, but general intelligence has no effect on the acquisition and espousal of evolutionarily familiar values and preferences. Individuals can often choose their values and preferences even in the face of genetic predisposition. One example of such choice within genetic constraint is circadian rhythms. Survey of ethnographies of traditional societies suggests that nocturnal activities were probably rare in the ancestral environment, so the Hypothesis would predict that more intelligent individuals are more likely to be nocturnal

than less intelligent individuals. The analysis of the
National Longitudinal Study of Adolescent Health (Add
Health) confirms the prediction.

In plain English, what they're saying is that genetic predisposition programs humans to wake with daylight and drift off
to sleep with nightfall; however, some humans have bucked that
and pushed through to be awake and productive after dark, and
the more intelligent individuals are more likely to be nocturnal
(night owls).

This particular study is the one that Mr. Kanazawa's article
in *Psychology Today* was based on. To expand on what's already
been stated, the study authors state that, while there is certainly a
genetic component to circadian rhythms, there is room for individual choices and decisions, suggesting that above-average IQ
in children is what drives them to fight to go to bed later, and
ultimately fall asleep later than their less intelligent counterparts.

So, when you're fighting one or more of your kids to get to bed
on time, just think, the one who drives you the most crazy is probably the smartest and will accomplish the most in life! See, there's a
silver lining to everything! (And yes, I have one of those…)

To conclude: *"Childhood IQ significantly increases nocturnal
behavior in early adulthood. More intelligent children are more likely
to grow up to be nocturnal adults who go to bed late and wake up late
on both weekdays and weekends."*

Night Owl MBA Students Achieve Higher Test Scores

Another study published in Elsevier's medical journal *Intelligence,* by researchers Davide Piffer, Davide Ponzi, Paola Sapi-
enza, Luigi Zingales, and Dario Maestripieri, shows that MBA

students who are night owls had significantly higher GMAT scores than their early riser counterparts.

Here's the study's abstract:

Individuals with a propensity to wake up early in the morning ("early-morning" types) and those who like to stay up late at night ("night owls") often exhibit distinctive psychological and physiological profiles. Previous research has shown that night owls score higher than early-morning people on different measures of cognitive ability and academic achievement. Baseline cortisol is one of the physiological variables associated with variation in chronotype and cognitive function. In this study we investigated whether a relationship between chronotype and performance is present also in the high range of intellectual ability and academic achievement, namely, among graduate students in a top-ranked MBA program in the US. In addition, we measured baseline cortisol levels in saliva samples collected in the early afternoon and analyzed them in relation to chronotype and GMAT scores. As predicted, GMAT scores were significantly higher among night owls than among early-morning types, regardless of sex. GMAT scores were also significantly higher among men than women, regardless of chronotype. Morningness eveningness was not significantly associated with variation in sleep amount or in undergraduate or graduate GPA scores, suggesting that the association between eveningness and high GMAT scores was not due to differences in study effort or skills. Sex, chronotype and baseline cortisol jointly accounted for 14% of the total variance in GMAT scores; baseline cortisol, however, did not mediate the effect of chronotype on GMAT scores. Consistent with the results of previous research, our study shows that the effects of chronotype

on cognitive ability and academic performance are rela-
tively small but detectable even among high-achieving
individuals. The mechanism linking eveningness and
high cognitive function remains unclear but the role of
personality traits and neuroendocrine function warrants
further investigation."

In discussing possible reasons for night owls being smarter
than early risers, the authors state:

According to the training effects hypothesis, evening
types have a frequent need to overcome the inconve-
niences of everyday life caused by conflicts with social
demands, (such as the daily schedules of academic institutions that are generally characterized by early starting
hours) and this need would in turn lead evening types to
develop higher problem solving abilities (Preckel et al.,
2011). Another explanation suggests that the association
between eveningness and greater cognitive function is a
by-product of the fact that night owls generally sleep less
than EM [early morning] types, and that more intelligent
people regardless of chronotype tend to require less sleep
due to more efficient neuronal recovery during nighttime. (Geiger, Achermann, & Oskar, 2010). Finally, it has
also been suggested that eveningness may have evolved by
sexual selection, because being active late in the evening
provided more opportunities for reproduction through
short-term mating (Piffer, 2010); in this view, the greater
intelligence of night owls might be related to their mating intelligence."

Or, to put it bluntly, night owls get laid way more than
morning people. Take that!

Regardless of which reason or hypothesis seems the most reasonable, there is no denying the fact that night owls are simply flat-out smarter and have higher intelligence than early riser counterparts. There is simply too much evidence to support that claim to even consider anything to the contrary.

Want to Get Ahead? Be a Night Owl!

While society loves to typecast us night owls as "unproductive" or "slothful," a 2009 study conducted by researchers at the University of Liege in Belgium monitored 15 extreme night owls and 16 extreme early birds in a lab. The volunteers had their brain activity measured an hour and a half after waking up, and again 10.5 hours after waking up.

In the morning test, the early birds and the night owls performed nearly the same in their responsiveness. But there was a gap at the 10.5-hour mark, at which time the night owls showed faster reaction times and were far more awake than the early birds.

This goes back to what I told you about friends who have been following a program of getting up at four or five o'clock in the morning in order to experience "extreme productivity," or whatever they call it. And if you remember, I had mentioned that these people were all morning types to begin with; they merely moved their waking time one to two hours earlier.

Without fail, they cannot last beyond two to three o'clock in the afternoon. On the phone you can hear them endlessly yawning, and on a web conference you can see the raccoon bags under their eyes and the general look of fatigue and sleep deprivation that is so easy to recognize nowadays, when so many people have it.

In many cases they've even told me that they're done for the day and need to wind down. At 2:00 p.m.! I mean, seriously, I'm just getting warmed up and beginning to hit my daytime peak at two o'clock.

Being mentally alert has a lot of uses, for example, having situational awareness on the road and therefore avoiding automobile accidents. However, for our purposes in this chapter, being mentally alert translates into having higher cognitive function and higher mental functioning. In other words, even if we're born equal, the night owl still comes out ahead of the early riser in the brainpower department.

Night Owls Are More Flexible with Work

Being able to "go the distance," as I like to put it, gives night owls yet another huge advantage in life over their early bird colleagues: Even though night owls must frequently adjust to an early morning schedule for work or school, they still thrive in those situations. And on top of that, night owls can adopt extended hours later in their day, or in other words, night owls not only work more effectively than early risers in the morning but can continue to do so all the way through to night!

This chapter obviously ties into the previous one because having higher intelligence will naturally equate to being more successful and enjoying a higher income. There are exceptions, of course, and there's little arguing that persistence alone has been the key to success for many. However, all else being equal, the night owls still come out on top.

Did you know that 37% of all automobile accidents are caused by drowsy motorists, according to a University of Pennsylvania study? This ties back into the correlation between morning rush hour, excessive drowsiness, and the aggressiveness that can come from caffeinism. Even minor sleep deficits can have huge effects. According to Juliette Franco of Stanford University, sleep loss generates a proportionate need for "sleep rebound."

Famous, Intelligent, Successful Night Owls

Want more proof that night owls have more brainpower? Here are some examples, from both the present and the past:

Alexis Ohanian, founder of Reddit: He told *Fast Company* he goes to bed around 2 a.m. and *tries* to get up by 10 a.m. Reddit is currently valued at approximately $1.8 billion, and Ohanian has made it onto the *Forbes* 30 Under 30 list two years in a row.

Elon Musk, founder of Tesla: Musk says he goes to bed around 1 a.m. He was a multimillionaire in his 20s, eventually became a billionaire, and Tesla now generates over $7 billion in annual revenue.

Barack Obama, 44th President of the United States: President Obama, during his eight years in the White House, went to bed around 1 a.m. each night and arrived for work in the Oval Office at 9 a.m. Regardless of your views on his politics and his presidency, few can argue the fact that merely getting to the Oval Office in the first place is perhaps the ultimate measure of success in American society, and he did it as a night owl.

Dharmesh Shah, founder of HubSpot: He says he goes to bed between 1:30 and 2:00 a.m. and sleeps around seven hours. He avoids early meetings and calls (as do I) and does not schedule anything before 11:00 a.m. Hubspot rakes in around $90 million in annual revenue.

Winston Churchill, former Prime Minister of the UK: Winston Churchill gets a lot of credit for the Allies prevailing in World War II, and rightly so. However, what most people don't know is that he was an extreme night owl, and in modern terms would likely be diagnosed has having delayed sleep phase disorder. Churchill got up at 11:00 a.m. and started his workday at noon, even during the war. His staffers became accustomed to having meetings with the Prime Minister in the bath, with the rest of the cabinet spread around the bathroom to take part, and they had to work for as long as he did every day.

Mark Zuckerberg, founder of Facebook: Routinely stays up until 6:00 a.m. Enough said. (Unsurprisingly, the first thing he does upon waking is check Facebook.)

There are many more, for example, J.R.R. Tolkien, Buzzfeed CEO Jonah Peretti, Box CEO Aaron Levie, Genius cofounder Tom Lehman, and more … the list could go on forever.

Morning Madness

Early rising doesn't make you smarter, it literally makes you dumber! Night owls consistently show higher intelligence and cognitive ability, at all hours of the day, over early risers. In addition, a disproportionate number of the people we consider highly successful happen to be night owls.

9

Night Owls Are More Productive

Want to Get More Done? Stay Up Later!

Hearing the words "early to rise" or being admonished by some "wiser" member of society—usually someone older who merely claims to also be wiser by default—to get up earlier and rise with the sun, or whatever the nonsense-du-jour happens to be, I cringe.

There's nothing more off-putting to a night owl than to have it in the back of our minds that we have to get up very early the next day. This is why we don't plan things that way. I know I personally have trouble sleeping if I have to get up early, which entirely defeats the purpose of "get up early to be more productive."

In addition, I experience an uncomfortable level of anxiety when I must get up earlier than my normal time. That's because, when you get up at your natural waking time, your adrenal glands pump out cortisol, the stress hormone, to wake you up. But when you get up before that happens, the cortisol spike occurs when you're already awake, hence the anxiety. And now that medical science has found that high cortisol levels—and not cholesterol—cause clogged arteries, it's downright harmful to our health, which will be covered in a later chapter.

No, we night owls don't plan to get up earlier to get more done. *We simply stay up later.*

After all, there's no good reason to fight nature, and science has shown us that our internal clocks are not a choice; they're given to us at birth and they're ours to use, or misuse, as we please. And besides, as previously mentioned, it'll shorten our lifespans.

If I've said it once, I'll say it a thousand times: Morning people I know—and that includes *every* morning person I know—simply cannot keep up with night owls past a certain point in the day. However, even though we may not like doing it, we can keep up with them if need be in the mornings. Studies have shown this as well. (Don't let this confuse you, though; studies showing that night owls suffer when forced to comply with a morning-centric schedule are still accurate, the difference being that *most night owls are not motivated* to try that early in the day. Or as *Fast Company* put it, "If early birds catch the worms, it's because the worm catching is rigged in their favor.")

Board-certified sleep specialist Dr. Michael Breus, author of *The Power of When: Discover Your Chronotype—and the Best Time to Eat Lunch, Ask for a Raise, Have Sex, Write a Novel, Take Your*

Meds, and More (Little, Brown and Company, 2016), in *Fast Company*'s "Work Smart" column online, has said, "In the normal, everyday workforce, the late-night people are assumed to be lazy because they can't get up and make it to early-morning meetings. They're assumed to be undisciplined."

Now we know damn well that we're not lazy—quite the contrary, actually—and we're certainly not undisciplined. After all, we're the ones with the higher incomes and higher IQs!

That description is certainly unfair, and of course is only an observation of Dr. Breus that he clearly disagrees with.

Likewise, he says he's constantly bombarded with people asking how they could get themselves to be up by four o'clock in the morning and get a hundred emails done by six o'clock and be off to a huge head start. However, he thinks this is the wrong question. His reasons are twofold: First, chronotypes are primarily determined by genetic predisposition, and, as we've seen, there's not much one can do to change their chronotype. Second, while being productive that early in the morning may seem ideal in our society, the truth is that you'll be exhausted by evening, which could hurt your personal life as well as your networking efforts. And what could be worse for business than flunking at networking?

He explains that a better approach is to embrace your chronotype rather than try to change it, and he tells employers that they really want both chronotypes in their workforce, albeit on the condition that they're lined up with the right duties. In other words, while a night owl account rep on the East Coast who has West Coast accounts and can sleep three hours later is in an ideal position, if it were reversed, the night owl would be miserable while an early riser would be ideal. It's all about putting people in the right positions, or more specifically, allowing them to work *with* their chronotype rather than *against* it.

Going back to Dr. Breus's constant bombardment with people asking how they can get up at four o'clock and be hyper-productive, aside from the fact that it is yet another example of living in a quick-fix society, where, for example, someone would rather just take a pill than see a therapist, it's also more evidence of the brainwashing we all suffer.

The brainwashing says that there's one, and only one, way to be productive: Get up earlier.

The fact that a board-certified sleep specialist, the kind who normally works with people who have severe intractable insomnia or some similar disorder, has patients coming to see him in search of a "quick fix" to get up several hours earlier and do a half-day's work in the process, goes to show just how deeply ingrained the brainwashing is, and how desperate people are to "fit in" and "be normal" by getting up early, just like their coworkers.

Then there's the obvious logical problem with the get-up-earlier-to-be-more-productive argument: There are 24 hours in the day, we all get the same 24 hours, and the times of day we choose to be productive are entirely irrelevant to our productivity.

One cannot dismiss the possibility that this desperation to magically get up earlier with the help of a sleep doctor may likely also come from the night owl sleep-shaming we've all had to deal with, and in many cases, myself included, have to deal with on an ongoing basis. Even when it seems that people finally get it, they don't get it. They demand to know why we can't be on a call at six o'clock in the morning. After all, in their minds, it's just a call. Or the misperception, even among family and friends, that we don't really work if we don't get up when society dictates that we do.

To us, getting up at 5:45 a.m. in order to make a 6 a.m. call is a downright nightmare, and I know from personal experience that when I've been in that situation, I slept very poorly, if at all, in anticipation of such a horror. Sadly, societal norms don't allow us to demand that *they* get on a 2:00 a.m. call (yes, I've actually done them). However, that is slowly but surely changing, and it's changing much more quickly outside the United States than inside, since the myth of the early riser is ingrained—nay, *brainwashed*—deeply into the fabric of American society.

Some years ago I had my first bout with lower back pain. This came as a surprise to me, and caught me off guard, because I was one of those rare people who had never experienced low back pain.

Then it came on suddenly and strongly. There was nothing structurally or physically wrong with me, there had been no automobile accident or other incident, and I tried self-hypnosis, relaxation breathing techniques, heat, ice, TENS machines, various pain-relieving creams, and on and on and on.

Finally, someone turned me on to a book entitled *Healing Back Pain: The Mind-Body Connection*, by Dr. John E. Sarno, MD (Warner Books, 1991). I could see that my back pain was being caused by internal tension that either had no other way out, or that didn't want to get out because the potential emotional turmoil might possibly be more than the mind and body want to deal with.

The pain went away merely with the understanding of what was causing the pain. To put it another way, there's no requirement to get rid of the tension or the external stressors that were causing that internal tension. Dr. Sarno referred to it as knowledge therapy.

The huge similarity between Dr. Sarno's book and this one is that both back pain and the legend of the early riser are uniquely American. It's only American society that celebrates the person who "goes it alone," the rugged individualist, the man on a mission.

He goes on to explain the epidemic of back, neck, and sciatic pain over the past several decades as being unique to America, and wonders if after millions of years, the American back has suddenly become deficient in just one generation?

What the book boils down to is that we're all exposed to stressors, sources of tension, repressed anger, repressed emotions, and much more. In other words, the demands of our uniquely American society, where the individual is not only encouraged, but actually expected, to achieve to a high degree without outside help, is the cause of much needless back, shoulder, neck, and buttock pain in this country. And it's all the result of tension that's become bottled up in muscles due to the pressure to succeed in our modern society.

Chronotypes and the Mind-Body Connection

If one were to choose what Dr. Sarno's greatest contribution was as a result of his work, it'd have to be the realization that there is indeed a mind-body connection, and, what's more, it's extremely powerful. No, it's all-powerful. In the case of back pain, along with fibromyalgia, it's been demonstrated via biopsy that the involved muscles are suffering mild ischemia, or oxygen deprivation. In the case of back pain, fibromyalgia, and other pains caused by the mind-body connection, which Dr. Sarno calls the tension myositis syndrome, or TMS, studies of biopsied muscle show an oxygen debt of anywhere from 1 to 5 percent. It doesn't take much to cause the pain, and the brain uses it as a way to distract us from even more painful emotional issues.

How does this relate to night owls and productivity? Simple: It shows that our minds and bodies are closely tied together, and doing something that throws the body out of whack will do the same to the mind.

Take this book, for example. A so-called "normal" person would get up at six or so, get to the office by eight, and start writing.

If I were to try that you'd be reading nonsensical gibberish. No, you wouldn't be reading anything, since the publisher wouldn't print my morning work product in the first place!

What actually works for me is to *get up when I naturally wake up.* Some days that happens at 7:00 a.m., other days at 9:30 a.m., and most days it's around 8:30 a.m., but regardless, what's important is that *I get up when my body decides it's time to wake me up* by hitting me with that jolt of cortisol. Once I'm awake I turn on my therapy light and read for a little while with my Great Dane, Mimi, at my feet, until the light's timer turns it off. I also use Philips Hue bulbs in the bedroom so I can change the color to bright daylight right from my iPhone, and down to a dark nightlight in the evenings.

Speaking of Philips Hue, their lights integrate with the excellent *Sleep Cycle* smartphone app, and you can set the app to gradually turn on your lights over 30 minutes prior to your alarm time in order to simulate sunrise, which is the most natural and healthful way to wake up. If I really need to get up early and use an alarm, that's what I use, not some horrible blaring alarm clock that will just generate more stress hormones! For a less expensive option, you can get an alarm clock with a built-in lamp that does the same thing.

Rather than follow some kind of regimented morning ritual, which seem to be all the rage these days (as P.T. Barnum said, there's one born every minute), I take my time, maybe have a cup of coffee if I feel the need (but I usually don't), go to the gym if it's a gym day, and if it's not I just ease into the day and get ready to head out the door when I'm ready.

Remember that it takes a full two hours for someone who is so-called "normal," meaning they have neither delayed sleep phase disorder (DSPD), which is characterized by the inability to fall asleep until extreme hours such as 4:00 or 5:00 a.m., or advanced sleep phase disorder (ASPD), which is characterized by people such as Apple CEO Tim Cook who brags about getting up at 3:45 a.m.; little does he know he doesn't have a choice in the matter and therefore has no bragging rights!

Considering the fact that it takes two hours to become fully awake and reach full cognitive function, what good would it do me to start writing any sooner than that?

Answer: *None.*

So, instead of the frantic morning rush most people are accustomed to, my mornings are more like "morning ease-ins." During those two hours I don't do anything requiring much brainpower, meaning I'll get my political news fix, make and enjoy breakfast and possibly coffee—the key word here being *enjoy*, not wolf down—then go and get in the shower and get dressed and be on my merry way. Since my youngest is still in preschool, some days I get to see her when she gets home around 11:15 a.m. before heading out to my office or wherever I may be headed.

And let me tell you, *she loves that.* If I had to give one, and only one, reason why I like taking my time in the mornings, that would be it.

(For the record, I absolutely *despise* the word "morning," and refer to it as "the a.m." instead, but that would get very tedious in a book.)

I recently read a book written by a big-name best-selling author that said if you want to achieve your goals, limit your time with your kids to 45 minutes a day.

What?!

That's fine if you want your kids to have issues as adults and be on psych meds and resent you, not to mention that those issues will cause the TMS pain Dr. Sarno described!

No, thank you, sir, I will choose to be present with my kids. One of the blessings of being self-employed is that I get to spend much more time with them than most dads do. In fact, they even made a point to tell me one day, together, that I'm the best dad of all their friends because I spend the most time with them.

I remember as a little kid when two of my close cousins told me the same thing about my dad. Being able to live with him and hear that from them melted my heart. And it's all because I refuse to follow society's dictates and absurd "success" advice to work so much that I'll never have the chance to see my kids!

You may be wondering by now how this relates to productivity, and the answer is simple.

Every day I'm in an amazingly great mood bordering on euphoria. And don't let yourself think money has anything to do with it, because I have only recently recovered from a dire financial crisis caused by medical issues (including the extreme adrenal exhaustion caused by that stupid "get up at four" book), along with a total ankle replacement that not only took me out of commission for several months but cost north of $300,000, and on top of that I didn't want to attempt to work from home while taking strong painkillers. Finally, and very ironically, quitting alcohol also contributed; without the booze and the hangovers, I suddenly had significantly more free time, and what do we do with extra free time? That's right, we find ways to spend money.

So if you think I'm borderline euphoric every day because I'm rolling in cash, think again. Sure, business and the economy are seriously on the upswing thanks to President Trump's tax plan, but don't think I'm happy because I'm loaded (with cash, not booze.) In fact just a couple of hours ago one of my senators personally called me on my cell phone, from *his* cell phone, asking for a campaign contribution because I've donated the max several times in the past, and I had to respectfully decline. He understood, and in fact the causes of those financial problems led to a very fruitful conversation.

Okay—with the money tangent out of the way, the simple answer is that *I'm extremely productive because I'm happy*, to the point of borderline euphoria.

Think about it: If you went into work every day so happy that you were almost giddy, full of excitement and bursting with enthusiasm, how long would it take for you to reach the top?

Probably not very long at all.

As Mr. Burns from the television series *The Simpsons* once said, albeit in an evil manner, "A happy worker is a productive worker."

So I ask again, why are employers forcing night owls to get up early and be specifically *unhappy*?

Another simple answer: It's the brainwashing. And may God help you if your boss is an early riser, or worse, a Tim Cook type with advanced sleep phase syndrome (ASPS), since they'll expect you to be up and at work when they are, and they'll shove their sleep-shaming down your throat until you're downright miserable, not to mention angry and resentful of your employer. Now how exactly does that help?

Natural Sleep Times = Happiness = Massive Productivity

By now we've established that having to get up too early makes us night owls very unhappy, and being able to operate on our natural schedule makes us very happy, for numerous reasons.

And that's one of the secrets of why night owls are more productive: Left to our own devices, without being forced to comply with societal norms, we become happy. And happiness equates to productivity.

In a study conducted in the UK by the Social Market Foundation and the University of Warwick's Centre for Competitive Advantage in the Global Economy, with Dr. Daniel Sgroi as the lead researcher, 700 subjects were chosen at random and were either shown a 10-minute comedy video or given a snack and a drink.

This was followed by a series of questions to ensure that the comedy clips actually did make the subjects happy. Once it was established that they were, they were given a series of tasks to measure their levels of productivity.

The result? Productivity in the happy group increased anywhere from 12%–20% over the control group.

Likewise, the researchers found a causal link between unhappiness and decreased productivity.

Dr. Sgroi said in his conclusion, "Having scientific support for generating happiness-productivity cycles within the workforce should ... help managers to justify work-practices aimed at boosting happiness on productivity grounds."

Or, to put it bluntly to employers, if you let your employees work on their natural schedule, the one that they're happy to abide by, you'll put more damn money in your pocket! Just think of all the economic crises and turmoil we've been through that could have possibly been avoided by allowing people to simply be happy at work, and therefore more productive. Even in good times, who doesn't want to have both productive and happy employees? Aren't companies graded on sites like Glassdoor. com on employee satisfaction? And won't a low grade keep the very best prospective employees away?

If you're still running your company based on the brainwashing, it's time for a refresh.

"Sleep Pressure" Gives Night Owls the Productivity Advantage

We may all get the same 24 hours in each day, but it's how we use those hours, or I should say, how many hours we use, that determines our ultimate productivity.

Sleep pressure is a term that refers to how long someone has been awake, and, you guessed it, studies have been done to explore the effects of sleep pressure on cognitive function.

In a study at the University of Liège in Belgium, conducted by doctoral student Christina Schmidt and led by Philippe Peigneux and published in the April 24, 2009, issue of *Science*, a group of early risers and a group of night owls were recruited to take alertness tests in a brain scanner. Subjects had to watch numbers on a computer screen and press a button anytime the numbers changed.

The subjects were allowed to sleep on their own natural schedules and they completed the test both 1.5 and 10.5 hours after waking, irrespective of the actual waking time.

Both groups performed equally well at 1.5 hours; however, at the 10.5-hour mark the night owls excelled and pulled ahead of their early riser counterparts. Not only that, but their reaction times actually improved compared to the early risers'.

The researchers concluded that once awake, sleep pressure builds up more quickly in early birds, and this hurts their cognition as the day goes on.

Night owls, on the other hand, did not experience any negative effects of sleep pressure; indeed, they actually improved in performance as the hours accumulated, and don't forget, they performed just as well as early birds at the 1.5 hour mark.

Based on that, it doesn't take a genius (or maybe it does?) to see why night owls are more productive: We simply don't burn out like early risers do, and instead we can go the distance.

Sleep researcher David Dinges of the University of Pennsylvania School of Medicine has said these results have "real-world consequences." He says that current methods of risk analyses for those in high-risk occupations such as airline pilots, that simply use time of day and number of hours worked to predict peak risk of accidents, must also take into consideration the fact that early risers lose concentration significantly more quickly than night owls.

So much for the brainwashing—and the myth of "early to bed and early to rise…."

Morning Madness

While society loves to slap labels such as "lazy" and "unproductive" on night owls, the truth is that we're far more productive than morning people, who have been proven to be unable to keep up with us as the day goes on. Night owls are also better choices for dangerous or high-risk occupations, since we do not lose concentration rapidly like early risers do.

10

Night Owls Are More Creative

Creativity Flourishes After the Early Birds Have Crashed

Birds. Crashing. Sorry, but that was just too easy! However, it's true: As you've already learned, morning people experience fewer productive hours each day, because they eventually crash while night owls keep going and going like the Energizer Bunny.

Early risers crash—both literally and figuratively. And the limited amount of useful hours they enjoy each day, versus the much greater amount enjoyed by night owls, also stifles their creativity.

In other words, if you want any sort of creative project done right, give it to a night owl. Or, wait…what you'll actually find is that highly creative people *are* night owls.

Seriously, who ever heard of a rock star getting up at five o'clock in the morning to work on that new song? Or the artist who set her alarm clock for four o'clock to "get ahead of the world" and work on that painting while everyone else is still sleeping?

Don't get me wrong: You will find those types of people working at those hours; however, it's because they never went to bed in the first place, not because they got up at some crazy early hour to get the job done.

As I've mentioned previously, I can wake up anywhere from 7:00 a.m. (rare) to 8:30 a.m. (my usual time) to as late as 11:00 a.m. (again rare). However, regardless of the fact that I happen to get up at 7:00 a.m. on some rare days—and when I was overdoing my thyroid medication, I was jumping out of bed at 5:45 a.m. bursting with energy—for some reason my brain doesn't come "online" until the afternoon. That's why I start writing at either 1 or 2 p.m. and don't even make the attempt any earlier. Granted, this is a fact- and science-based book, but even then, it takes some level of creativity to put decades of research and hundreds of individual pieces of research and science into one coherent work. Not to mention all that damn medical jargon I had to learn to even *understand* what the research is saying (thankfully my inner science geek has a fetish for reading medical books so it wasn't *that* bad).

I've also mentioned previously that my wife is one of those rare people who have come to understand and accept that I'm a night owl, I was born that way, and will always be that way. I'm also certain this was difficult for her to come to accept having been raised by a military dad who didn't stand for sleeping in. Then again, having said that, we know that chronotypes are largely genetic, so it wasn't her upbringing that makes her get up early as much as her parents' genes. (Although rising early as a matter of genetics rather than of choice makes it even more difficult for early risers to understand us; they simply assume that getting up early is the norm for all people. This is why I give my wife so much credit for coming to accept that part of me.)

Looking back—way back—I can remember my seventh-grade English teacher talking to me one day and saying, with a slight wink, that people like us who have trouble getting out of bed early are smarter than the rest.

Well, we've already established that, backed by science, so let's move on to the reasons why night owls are more creative. So much so, in fact, that morning people not only admit the same but also have even mocked and ridiculed creative, night owl types as "freaks" or "weirdos." Believe me, I've heard it myself. People who know that I'm both a night owl and an author nearly always assume that I spend my life writing books late at night. Little do they know that I spend a month or two a year writing and spend the rest of the time serving my consulting clients.

Every now and then I come across one of those "Windows or die" type of people who can't stand the fact that all of my computers are Macs and have been since 2003. Inevitably they say something to the effect of, "Macs are only for creative work like graphic design, and for business you need Windows." Aside from the fact that they all missed the memo that it's not 1996 anymore, they sometimes throw in, "And since you like to stay up late and get up late you must be one of those creative types."

Of course, in this context, "creative type" is used as a pejorative. They're trying to imply that I must be some type of weirdo who showers once a month and stays up all night, huddled over my laptop writing books. It seems that tons of people hold this misconception, despite the fact that they know I'm a business book author—or in this case, we'll just say nonfiction—and that the overwhelming majority of my time is spent running my businesses and not writing books.

Also inevitably, these are generally the same people who say, "I wish I could become an author, but I just can't write a book."

Getting published is one thing, but in my opinion, anyone who can write a blog post can write a book. Take Mark Cuban, for instance. His book, despite being one of the better I've ever read, is actually just a collection of his blog posts over the years. He frankly admits that he doesn't have the patience to sit down and write a book so that's what he did.

However, the morning types don't seem to think they can, despite the fact that the business book market is loaded with early riser authors.

Is it because—gasp—*they aren't creative?* (Secret: No creativity is required to write nonfiction as it's all based in fact.)

Science Doesn't Know Why, but Confirms We're More Creative

Italian researchers from the Department of Psychology at the Catholic University of the Sacred Heart in Milan say that while science isn't fully understanding of why night owls are more creative, they suggest it could be due to adapting to living outside the norm.

"Being in a situation which diverges from conventional habit, nocturnal types often experience this situation, may encourage the development of a nonconventional spirit and of the ability to find alternative and original solutions," said Professor Marina Giampietro, lead author of the study.

(Side note: The study authors, in describing the study, which consisted of 120 people who are either morning people or night people, also said that both types are very rare and that most people fall somewhere in between. Apparently they haven't been forced to live and work in the United States and experience our machismo nonsense about who gets up earliest if they believe that!)

Once each subject was categorized as morning or night types, they underwent three different and distinct tests to measure creative thinking. The first test asked the subjects to draw a picture based upon an image shown to them by the researchers. The second test consisted of adding lines to create complete objects on a piece of paper containing only individual curved and straight lines. Finally, they were asked to do the same but instead were given 30 pairs of vertical lines to work with.

The result? Night types excelled on every single individual test, and aced all three. Of all the morning types, on the other hand, not a single one scored more than 50 on any single solitary one of the tests!

The study also found that creativity did not decline with age, and in fact it persists as people continue to age.

At Washington State University, professor Hans Van Dongen, at their Sleep and Performance Research Center, further explored the differences between morning and night types.

He believes the fact that night types are more creative has a lot to do with the fact that night owls are far more extroverted than either evening or "intermediate" types, or in plain English, the people who don't technically fall into either category.

He goes on to say there may be a link between the personality trait of being an extrovert and heightened creativity. My own life as a night owl confirms this. Even if the intellectual, cognitive centers of my brain are fully capable of logical thinking and the execution of tasks in the morning alongside the best of the night owls, my creative side doesn't light up until later on. And the later it gets, the more it lights up. That's a big reason why I have trouble falling asleep any earlier than midnight, and even when I go to bed then, it's because I'm either very tired, or am forcing myself to do so.

In a 2009 paper from the London School of Economics, it was proposed that daylight-based schedules are a societal convention, and it takes a high IQ to think of new ways of structuring one's days. According to the report, we're the beneficiaries of evolution, and come from a long line of ancestors who used the daylight hours to get work and other stuff done, and that it takes an intelligent and creative individual to buck that trend and try a daily routine that goes against our evolutionarily programming. In other words, night owls are innovators.

The Sales Training Flunkout Who Became a Top Sales Rep

I can remember it vividly even though it's been over 20 years: The day I got the call to inform me that I'd been offered the position I had been waiting for, for over two years—my dream sales job.

While I was excited to spend those three weeks learning all I needed to learn to excel at that job—and dupe my employer into sending me home for one weekend on the excuse that I had to check on my dog, when in reality it was for an AC/DC concert—I was disappointed to find that there wasn't very much sales training at all, but rather product training.

One thing I will say, however, is that this was the three weeks of training that led me to the best sales manager I ever had, the one who helped me to become a top sales pro, and without that experience I wouldn't be a published author and wouldn't be writing this book today.

While I loved that sales manager for his disbelief in the magic of cold calling, what I loved about the sales trainer during those three weeks was that he said the same thing. He explained that while cold calling would've worked 20 years earlier (meaning the 1970s, based on when that training occurred), nowadays people will just shut you down and you have to find new, and better, and *more creative* ways to prospect.

After that training ended, my new boss explained why cold calling is a waste of time, paired me up with the top sales rep in the office, and the rest is history. First I released my online e-course in 2003 and quit my last job ever only six weeks later, and then *Never Cold Call Again: Achieve Sales Greatness Without Cold Calling* (Wiley, 2006) spent a week at #1 on Amazon and immediately hit the *New York Times* best-seller list.

But the question is, with so many other reps in that same office, not to mention all the reps who came and went thanks to the sales profession's notoriously high turnover, why was it *me* who succeeded and "cracked the code" on how to get leads and sales without cold calling?

Looking back, I was the only night owl in the office that I'm aware of. That top sales rep was a morning person, although it was for mostly practical reasons: He arrived at 7:00 a.m. so he could be home by 4:00 p.m. and get plenty of time in with his kids. (That "success" author who said anything more than 45 minutes a day with your kids is a waste of productive work time should read this!)

If I was the only night owl in the office, *and* I was the only person who, despite everyone receiving the same guidance from our sales manager, managed to find entirely new ways to get leads and sales without cold calling, *perhaps* it's because I was the only night owl?

And because night owls are more creative?

In any case, that's the reason why I don't even bother attempting to work on a book such as this until at least an hour past noon. Otherwise I wind up reading my work in the afternoon—when my brain is "on"—and inevitably delete any and all work I'd written in the morning.

Similarly, when my wife goes to bed at 10 or 11 at night, I can readily grab my laptop, open it up, and the words start flying without the routine of sitting down at my office desk and getting my mind in the writing zone.

But I digress. Let's talk about that top sales rep—the one who missed sales training.

He was an extrovert for sure. Despite the fact that the hotel where our training was being held was somewhat remote, about two hours north of San Francisco, he still called a cab most nights and found some party somewhere.

Every day he'd show up at starting time, 8:00 a.m.—I don't know how—and would be in his characteristic dark sunglasses, which served two purposes. First, it was to hide his bloodshot, hangover eyes from the rest of the class. Second, it was so he could sleep through class!

That's right, we weren't being graded or anything like that, and while the sales trainer was excellent, he was still just someone who just wanted to go home at five o'clock, so he didn't care.

We'd get silly assignments where we would be handed a spec sheet that was completed by a hypothetical customer, stating what features they required, how many voicemail boxes, how many phones and lines, and so on. Then we had to program all of this despite the fact that we were up there to learn how to *sell* the stuff, not how to *program* it—after all that's why the company employed technicians! And to make matters worse, if any of us got caught programming so much as a single speed dial onto a customer's phone, the technicians would file a union grievance, even though we were trying to save our customer the needless $200 visit fee plus the one-hour, $150 minimum on top of it. And to think they're filing union grievances all because the sales reps—you know, those of us who generate the money to pay their salaries—wanted to avoid having customers fuming at us over paying $350 to get a speed dial programmed and never buying from us again.

(If you're not in sales and wondering what the big deal is, it's because it's a basic tenet of sales knowledge that it's far easier to sell more stuff to an existing customer than it is to find a new one—but not if the company is screwing them with service fees.)

Having said all that, if some jerk negotiated the price down to nothing, I'd tell him to call the 800 number then quickly hang up. My full-price customers, on the other hand, got the red carpet service from me. This is precisely why I'm not one of *those* people who try to haggle price on everything.

Another example of corporate stupidity aside, this was something our party-animal friend simply couldn't do. Nor did he bother. Everyone knew he missed all of yesterday's class and had no clue how to do any of this, so he didn't. He continued to cruise through the three weeks, staying out all hours while we were confined to karaoke nights in the bar lounge. (Seriously, it was that bad.)

We all left assuming he'd crash and burn when it came time to perform.

But he didn't.

In fact, he excelled. He kicked everyone's butt, at least until I got my own creative juices going and finally caught up with him and then passed him.

Before explaining why he excelled, it can probably be summed up in five words: *He is a night owl.*

He excelled in large part because he was a big extrovert. Which makes sense when you consider that it really does fit the party-animal persona. You can have someone who is up at the crack of dawn, studies ferociously during training, does all the right things, and still falls flat—because the person is introverted, and as I've told people probably hundreds of times, social skill is what matters in the real world. That's how I succeeded despite being a college dropout and yet managed to hold jobs requiring college degrees.

The other reason those crack-of-dawn people don't excel despite doing everything right—or in this case, showing up at all!—is because of a relative lack of creativity.

Despite being teamed up with the office's top sales rep to learn the ropes, I still had to undergo a few years' worth of trial-and-error effort to figure out how to *really* find *really* hot leads without cold calling—at all. Which, if you think about it, makes sense, considering the fact that leads generated by cold calls have the absolute lowest percentage of converting to actual sales. (If you're wondering, referrals have the highest closing rate of all leads at anywhere from 70 to 90%. That's why if you're new in sales, or in a new industry, you should be hitting two to three networking events *every single weekday.*)

And believe me, creative doesn't even begin to describe the lengths to which I went in order to find new and novel ways to get leads without cold calling. Not to mention that I was also living the party-animal lifestyle. I mean, when I started that job I was 23 years old, single, and living in Las Vegas. Who under those circumstances wouldn't go out every night? Or at least five nights a week, anyway. More reason why I designed a sales system that didn't require me to get up early! Instead of having to do the prospecting work myself, I created systems to do it for me.

I can't remember how many nights I'd get home at six, hammer a ton of coffee, get ready and dressed, and be at work by nine or so. That's why I was so hellbent on finding a way around it. And I did.

The reason why? Creativity. A morning-centric, less-creative, and more "by the book" type of person would do what I had tried and failed at: Reading every book and listening to every audio on the topic of getting sales, then trying those methods only to repeatedly fall flat on my face, not realizing that the world was at the onset of the Information Age and that cold calling, if it worked poorly before, wasn't working much at all anymore.

Similarly, I forced myself out to lots of networking functions, and my inner extrovert came out. For all of my life I'd been known as an introvert, and assumed I was one myself, but maybe a lifetime of having to get up early in the morning was causing that? Once I found ways to make my hours more flexible, I also found myself being massively more outgoing with people.

Now it's a joke amongst friends that I'm "the shy one." Ha! And to think that I really was shy once upon a time, or perhaps the early rising was making me that way. After all, how extroverted and outgoing can you be when you're physically and mentally exhausted all the time?

Now enough about me and back to that drunken yet amazing sales pro. He obviously did well in sales in large part due to his extroversion.

Having said that, I'd also like to suggest that he excelled in no small part due to his *creativity*.

I obviously had to tap large creative stores to find my ultimate lead-generation system, which I first used for myself and later sold to others, and in fact that's an ongoing process as times change and the number of tools available online and via apps continues to explode exponentially.

I also know that this top sales pro didn't cold call. No top sales pros cold call, but that's not how I knew. I knew by observation. However, like most top sales pros, he wasn't very keen on sharing his secrets and would jokingly and dismissively tell everyone else to get out there and "bang doors" if they wanted to make it big, something I'd also do only a short time later, after having given up on enlightening them.

Not knowing what he was actually doing, and knowing that he wasn't related to the boss or anything like that, looking back I have to assume that his methods were either the same, or very similar, to what I ended up doing. Those methods consisted of a collection of self-marketing activities organized into one master system, which I refer to as the "system of systems." (Get a copy of *Never Cold Call Again* for more info if you're in sales and want to get out of cold calling hell.)

Thus far, we've concluded that our party-happy sales rep excelled because he's extroverted, and because he's creative, both of which tie back into being a night owl, for extroversion and creativity are both hallmarks of the night owl personality.

Author Stereotypes versus Author Truths (or Entrepreneurial Truths)

I'd known my friend and fellow Internet entrepreneur Mike Filsaime for a few years when I went for a visit to his former offices in New York to meet up and brainstorm.

Prior to launching his Internet business and making millions in a product launch in 2006 that continues to fuel his existing businesses, Mike was a sales manager at a Toyota dealership.

On that particular visit, I met Mike's former boss at the Toyota dealer. He'd come to learn how he could also get out of the car business and into the world of being self-employed and free of a job forever.

The former boss told me all about how for the longest time, Mike would come into work in the mornings with dark raccoon circles under his eyes, totally exhausted but seemingly exhilarated.

It turns out that he stayed up all night—every night—working on his Internet business. And once that business took off, he finally quit the job.

Here's the thing: Being a sales manager at a Toyota dealership doesn't take much creativity. It's more of a nuts-and-bolts, managing the numbers type of job, though the marketing aspect of it requires some creative skill, and that's a big reason Mike did so well at it.

However, starting an Internet business—nay, merely coming up with an idea for one—does in fact require creativity. Lots of it. As does deciding how to position the product, how to market it, what the selling points are, which buyer triggers it will hit, and so much more that most people never see behind the scenes.

And to this day, Mike is one of those guys who can stay up all night, working away at whatever new idea is on his mind.

Another friend of mine makes more money than anyone I know, as far as I know. His name is Armando Montelongo of *Flip This House* fame, and according to *Forbes*, his annual income is approximately $70 million and his net worth is over $200 million. That was a few years ago, so I'm sure it's even higher now.

Armando has the unique ability to have an idea flash into his mind, haul ass to his office, say on a Friday afternoon for example, and not come out until Sunday...without any sleep. It very much reminds me of how I created my first online product that went on to cause so many more successes to follow.

Come to think of it, with few exceptions, nearly all Internet entrepreneurs I know are hardcore night owls. Like me, their primary motivation in starting a business was to break free of a job and the chains of being forced to live on an early morning schedule.

Meanwhile, you've heard me note that nearly all research showing that being a night owl is nonoptional and something we cannot change, along with most studies showing night owls to be smarter, more creative, with more endurance, and so on, coming from overseas. However, there is one exception: Silicon Valley.

While the rest of the world is enlightened to the strong advantages of flexible, night-owl-friendly work schedules for the benefit of both employer and employee, the United States is still stuck in a very 1950s machismo game of insisting that the world start in the early morning and that all of its citizens must comply or they won't prosper. (We who have to live our lives as night owls consider it a particularly sick and twisted game.)

However, in Silicon Valley, flexible work schedules are all the rage. Extreme morning types are allowed to come in at five o'clock if they so wish, and night owls are permitted to start at noon if they so wish.

The result? The area has produced, and continues to produce, some of the most cutting-edge technological breakthroughs the world has ever seen. In fact I'm using one right now.

So why isn't the rest of America following suit?

One of the main reasons I feel qualified to answer this question is due to my years-long befuddlement at why people get so furious and downright angry for advocating against cold calling in my work as a sales author and consultant.

I've come to realize and understand that these people are not arguing in favor of cold calling because of experiential reasons, or actual results, or some other proof that it works.

No, they're so passionate about it because they have a *strong emotional attachment* to cold calling.

Just as followers of any certain religion will naturally want to argue why it's the one true religion and why others should join them, it's the emotional connection that compels them to do so.

It's the words the cold callers use to argue their point that gives away their emotional connection, things like, "You have to get out there in the trenches," and "You have to fight the good fight," and "There are no shortcuts" are evidence that they are emotionally attached, and that they have no logical or rational explanation, let alone results or numbers.

Likewise, those who have lived their lives being forced to be up before dawn to sit in traffic for an hour and be at work by 8:00 a.m. (or earlier) seem to believe it's somehow "unfair" that we move to flexible work hours and they will have to see a younger generation being "lazy" and coming into work at—gasp!—10:00 a.m.!

CEOs and the Perpetual Myth of the Early Riser

Before going any further, I want to make sure you don't get me wrong politically. When I complain about the way people think in America, I'm strictly referring to the uniquely American attachment to early rising, and it's probably no coincidence that the morning myth was created by one of our nation's Founding Fathers. The same is true if I seem critical of CEOs. The truth is that I have the utmost respect for the horrifically long hours and extreme levels of stress they are forced to endure, and while many will disagree, I believe their eight-figure annual incomes are fully justified in light of that.

Think about it: While the company's employees are at church or their kids' games or at a barbecue with friends on a Sunday, the CEO is being interrogated on some television news show as to why the stock dropped one-tenth of one point in the previous week. When a product is found to be defective or even dangerous, it's the CEO who is the public face of the company, taking all of the arrows while the employees are enjoying a typical 8-to-5 workday or a relaxing weekend or vacation.

Considering all of that, in the best interests of both the shareholders and the employees, CEOs should probably be paid *more*, not less!

In any case, in my years of reading about this topic of morning people versus night owls, which has always greatly interested me, and in my research for this book, I kept coming across article after article that all seemed to be written for no other purpose than to remind us that America's CEOs get up and get to work at extremely early hours.

On one hand, some probably believe they may have to, given their heavy workloads. However, since we all get the same 24 hours in a day, that idea is easily disproven.

The more likely probability is that they're early risers because they've always been early risers. And as you now know, the only reason the early bird gets the worm is because the system is rigged in favor of the early bird. That's why they perform better, on paper at least, in school and at work. It's because those particular activities happen to start in the morning, usually at eight o'clock to be specific, when a night owl's brain is still mush but the early bird's brain is already "on."

Before moving forward, let's get one thing straight: *CEOs are* not *entrepreneurs.*

Sure, some started out that way—for example, Mark Zuckerberg, who doesn't go to bed until six in the morning many days. He's an extreme night owl to be sure.

Then there's Jeff Bezos, who now gets up at insanely early hours, but Mark Cuban recalls seeing him post in forums at all hours of the night, back when he was forming Amazon, asking for all sorts of advice, from starting an affiliate program to building an e-commerce backend to you name it. It would seem that he may have been a night owl as an entrepreneur but must now stick to a morning-centric schedule as a CEO.

And of course there's my favorite, Apple CEO Tim Cook. He's not my favorite CEO, mind you, just my favorite one to pick on. This is the guy who sends out tweets bragging that he was up at 3:45 a.m. or whatever insane hour his advanced sleep phase syndrome (ASPS) had him up at. I still can't figure out if this guy is trying to sleep-shame everyone else, or if he saw the science showing that such extreme early rising is trashing his adrenals and shortening his lifespan and he's just acting out.

The fact of the matter is that CEOs are early risers because most happen to be older and members of a generation in which people live and die by early rising. "Never let the sun catch you in bed," was the mantra they grew up with.

Fast-forward to today and you have the management ranks of virtually all companies populated by early risers, particularly upper management and the C-suite. These people know they had to get up early to climb the corporate ladder—the ladder that's rigged for early risers—and expect the same of everyone else. You can almost hear them sounding like whiny children, with a big fat, "But it's just not *fair* that those younger guys can sleep later than I did!"

And the emotional, rather than logical or rational, attachment to early rising unfortunately continues to persist.

Bezos, Explained

As a fitting conclusion to this chapter—and perhaps thanks to good luck, because this particular interview occurred only a few weeks prior to writing this—I'd like to share some details of an interview with Jeff Bezos conducted by the Economic Club of Washington, DC.

I'll give away the best part right up front: In the interview, Bezos admitted that he avoids afternoon meetings like the plague because he simply doesn't have the brainpower in the afternoon that he does in the morning.

That goes to show something I've already shared with you, the fact that while early birds start, well, early, they simply cannot go the distance. They hit a wall and crash while the night owls keep going and going like the Energizer Bunny. To add insult to early bird injury, night owls can perform just as well cognitively in the mornings if forced to do so.

To quote Bezos, "I like to do my high IQ meetings before lunch. Anything that's going to be really mentally challenging— that's a 10 o'clock meeting. Because by 5:00 p.m., I'm like, 'I can't think about that today. Let's try this again tomorrow at 10 o'clock.'"

Or, in other words, like all early risers, Bezos has fewer truly useful hours available in each day compared with night owls. This is especially confirmed by the fact that he gets a full eight hours' sleep every night.

"I think better, I have more energy, my mood is better—all these things," he explains, regarding the eight hours of sleep. He continues, "And think about it: As a senior executive, what do you really get paid to do? You get paid to make a small number of high-quality decisions. Your job is not to make thousands of decisions every day. Is that really worth it if the quality of these decisions might be lower because you're tired or grouchy or any number of things?"

Hmm. That last question he posed goes right back to the fact that the system is rigged in favor of early risers. He assumes that it's okay for *him* to get eight hours of sleep so he's not tired or grouchy, but what about those who are tired and grouchy in those 10 o'clock meetings because they're night owls who couldn't fall asleep until two in the morning?

Sadly, one of the many articles reporting on this interview with Bezos declares his early rising and 10 o'clock meetings as absolute requirements for success, and so the morning myth continues.

Morning Madness

The connections science has made between night owl tendencies and increased creativity, intelligence, productivity, and so much more have been proven, yet our morning-centric society continues to insist on defying them and continues to perpetuate the morning myth. And despite all that, Jeff Bezos, the richest man in the world at the time of this writing, admits that he crashes in the afternoon and can't think at all past five … and he's an early riser.

CHAPTER

11

Night Owls Are More Relaxed

Getting Up Early Is Stressful (but You Already Knew That)

In the example of 24 circadian rhythms discussed in a previous chapter, you learned that it's a rush of cortisol—the body's stress hormone that is produced by the adrenal glands, two walnut-sized glands that sit atop each kidney—that naturally wakes us each day.

The key word here is "naturally"—I personally suffer from a strong sense of anxiety when I have to get up unusually early, and it's that rush of cortisol, that comes at my body's natural waking time, that causes it.

I used to belong to a group called the Dallas Business Alliance, and it was so good that I was a member despite the weekly 7:30 a.m. meetings. (Thankfully the meetings were really close to home.) It was also good for Dubya encounters, meaning George W. Bush; his office is in the same building where we met and he showed up at 7:30 a.m. every day. That's part of how I managed to snag so many selfies with him. I also had Rotary Club of Dallas meetings on Wednesdays, at noon.

However, I was a quivering mess of anxiety on Wednesdays, and I crashed early and crashed hard.

The cause of the anxiety was getting up at 6:15 a.m. in order to get ready and get dressed for my weekly "suit day"; Dallas Business Alliance was held at one of those private social clubs in the Park Cities area of Dallas (read: wealthy) where wearing jeans would cause the entire time-space continuum to collapse while people whose age had to be in the triple-digits would raise all hell about it.

Remember the many times I've said my natural rising time, notwithstanding variables such as a night of insomnia, is typically around 8:30 a.m.?

Well, one hour into our meeting every Wednesday, that rush of cortisol would hit me like a ton of bricks (or rather like a ton of caffeine and ephedrine, combined), and that, combined with the amount of coffee I drank to get going that early, would literally have my hands shaking.

On top of that I was always sweating profusely under my suit. For that reason I invested in talc and undershirts, and they worked; however, an undershirt in the already brutal Dallas summer heat isn't particularly amusing later in the day.

We adjourned at nine, I went to my office, and eventually found that I had to listen to an anti-anxiety self-hypnosis audio, or attempt to meditate. After about two and a half hours at the office, it was time to go back to the car to get to my Rotary meeting. There I'd have even more coffee to get through at least the next few hours.

Then, by mid-afternoon, like Amazon's esteemed CEO and the richest man in the world, I crashed. And I crashed hard.

Relaxed? I was anything but relaxed!

I was stressed, and to explain why, I'm going to describe how coffee works to give you "energy"—or does it?

Coffee and Getting Up Too Early: Both Are Major Stressors

My decision to get off caffeine came after reading the excellent book *Caffeine Blues: Wake Up to the Hidden Dangers of America's #1 Drug* by Stephen Cherniske (Grand Central Publishing, 2008).

As Cherniske explains in great detail in the book, there's a common misperception that caffeine gives one energy, but in reality what it does is give one stress. The perceived "energy" is merely how we perceive that stress.

As mentioned, cortisol is the body's stress hormone. The body releases it in response to stress, or to perceived danger. Its purpose in our bodies is to activate the fight-or-flight response, which, for example, would activate when one of our ancestors would be out picking berries for the tribe's dessert that evening when a hungry grizzly bear would suddenly appear from out of nowhere. What cortisol does in order to prepare the body for a potential fight is to increase heart rate and pump more blood to muscles and limbs, increase the clotting ability of blood in case of injury, and create a heightened sense of focus and awareness. These are cortisol's primary purposes in the fight response.

As to the flight response, again, the increased blood flow to muscles and limbs will allow one to run faster and harder from a threat versus attempting to do so in a normal state.

This was all well and good back in the caveman days, but in our modern society, we're exposed to stressors our bodies have not yet adapted to and all sorts of health problems have resulted.

Take George W. Bush, for example. Not too long after I moved to Dallas he was in the same hospital where I had my ankle replacement done because his arteries were found to be 95% blocked and he needed emergency surgery to clear them and avoid heart attack and stroke.

The big question everyone was asking was, how did someone with such an extremely healthy lifestyle end up with clogged arteries? After all, the man eats healthy, takes care of himself, runs every morning (or did before his knee replacements; now he cycles), and so on. So what happened?

What happened is that serving eight years as President of the United States, very likely the number one most stressful job in the world, exposed his body to an onslaught of virtually non-stop cortisol, especially after 9/11 and the two wars that ensued.

Many people find this hard to believe, and when they do, I tell them to go find a new doctor. Mine doesn't care much about cholesterol, other than wanting me to maintain a high level of HDL, or "good" cholesterol. That's because his high fees are earned. He's one of the best in the business, and is fully aware that the lipid hypothesis, the thing that started all this hysteria over cholesterol, has been disproven.

The truth is that diet cannot possibly have any effect on cholesterol levels. That's because if you eat cholesterol, the body uses what it needs, if any, and the rest goes out. (Pick a number as long as it's number 1 or number 2!) The reality is that the liver synthesizes cholesterol as needed and removes excess cholesterol from the blood.

Stress is the real cause of clogged arteries. Going back to the evolutionary role of cortisol, few of us obviously live in any real danger anymore. That's why so many people are into extreme sports such as skydiving and bungee jumping. It's because at some evolutionary level, our bodies actually expect danger, and many people fulfill that expectation in such ways.

However, while not literally dangerous, the normal day-to-day stressors of modern life are indeed harmful to our health thanks to the cortisol response they produce.

Our ancestors thousands of years ago would find their hearts pounding rapidly in response to that grizzly bear, or an attacker, or some other real and present danger. However, have you noticed that your heart does the same exact thing, say, when you're deeply worried about money? Or when you're waiting for that dream job offer and the phone rings?

These aren't real threats to life, but they are nevertheless perceived as such by the body, which in turn produces a cortisol response.

In the case of coffee, it doesn't actually provide energy. What it in fact does is stimulate the adrenal glands to produce cortisol and norepinephrine, which in turn cause the stress response in your body. Because the cortisol–stress response heightens awareness—so that you can detect danger, focus, win the fight, and so on—people experience this and confuse it with actual energy.

If it were indeed actual energy, there wouldn't be such a pronounced crash as there is with coffee for most people. The crash comes after the excess cortisol has been removed from your bloodstream. Your adrenals go offline because you overstimulated them with coffee and they need rest, and so you "crash."

If you're a natural night owl like me and follow the advice in a book to get up at four or five in the morning, or in the case of Dallas Business Alliance, 6:15 a.m., you're hit with a major double-whammy when you get the jolt of cortisol at your natural waking time on top of the excess cortisol already present from the coffee! It's no surprise, then, that I endured the horrific experience of adrenal exhaustion after trying to do the early riser thing for not very long.

Considering all of this, it's no wonder that I was a quivering mess of anxiety on those early days. And the fact that night owls who are able to actually live on their natural schedules don't have to deal with all of this is why they're more relaxed overall.

Cortisol Keeps Early Risers on Edge

A research team at the University of Westminster had 42 volunteers take saliva samples eight times throughout the day for two days, starting when they woke up, regardless of what time that happened to be.

In the case of the earliest early bird, waking time was 5:22 a.m., and it was 10:37 a.m. in the case of the nightiest night owl.

Lab results from the saliva samples showed that those who were early risers—defined as rising before 7:21 a.m.—had the highest rates of cortisol. What's more, their cortisol levels remained high all day. The researchers had yet to discover whether the high cortisol levels caused the early birds to wake early, or whether early rising was the cause of the high cortisol levels.

Either way, it's bad news for early birds any way you look at it, because cortisol is one nasty, ugly hormone to have hanging around in excess.

Implications of Heightened Cortisol Levels

Chronic stress, which is defined as having chronically high cortisol levels—remember, it's the body's stress hormone—is associated with depression, increased susceptibility to illness and infections, arterial stiffness, high blood pressure, osteoporosis, diabetes, obesity, anxiety, and so many more bad things.

For an example, consider someone who has been on prednisone, or another corticosteroid, for an extended period of time. Prednisone and other drugs like it mimic the effects of cortisol in the body. It can be a miracle drug when used appropriately (for example, in patients with rheumatoid arthritis), but it carries a long list of horrible side effects when used long-term.

These long-term side effects mimic the effects of excess cortisol production in the body. They include glaucoma, cataracts, fluid retention, high blood pressure, psychological problems such as problems with mood, memory, and other issues, weight gain, suppressed immunity, thinning of skin, slower wound healing, and more.

And that's what chronic high cortisol does to a person. It's akin to taking prednisone for a long time without realizing that you're doing it, or worse, being unknowingly poisoned with it over a long period of time.

Cortisol and the University of Westminster Study

Going back to the study just mentioned, the research team did a 10-week follow-up study, and found that early risers reported far more muscle aches, cold and flu symptoms, headaches—and *significantly worse moods*—than night owls.

(Important note: When you see the word "significant" in reference to any medical study, or elsewhere in this book, it isn't just an adjective I'm throwing around. It refers to *statistical significance*, something marketers like myself live and die by when doing marketing tests. In simple terms it means that the outcomes were different enough and far enough outside the margin of error to reliably predict the same results in the general population.)

The lead researcher, Dr. Angela Clow, said, "This work is interesting because it may provide a physiological basis for the often-reported difference between early and late risers.

"Early awakening was associated with greater powers of concentration, being busier and experiencing more hassles throughout the day as well as reporting more anger and less energy at the end of the day.

"On the other hand, late wakers were more leisurely and less busy.

"It is possible that cortisol may contribute toward these differences in temperament, as it is known to be able to influence mood and concentration."

According to Neil Douglas of the Scottish National Sleep Centre, peak cortisol levels occur in most people by 8:00 a.m. In other words, our typical workday starting time of eight o'clock is two hours too early.

Oh, and speaking of sleep, chronically high cortisol levels cause insomnia and poor sleep quality. Early risers may continue to rise early even after the need subsides, just like President Bush does, because perhaps they simply cannot sleep even if they try.

Morning Madness

Studies have proven that early rising, whether by choice or by force, causes chronically elevated cortisol levels, the stress hormone that wreaks havoc on the body when it's hanging around but not actually needed. The hormone is also linked to depression, anxiety, and significantly worse moods when it's elevated, which is the case all day long with early risers…perhaps that's why they're so cranky all the time?

12

Night Owl Discrimination and Sleep-Shaming

The Time Has Come to End Discrimination Against Night Owls

When I said that early birds get the worm because society has the system rigged in their favor, or rather quoted the same, I wasn't kidding. Early risers in our society have an artificial advantage by virtue of the fact that they're most awake and alert at precisely the same times that work and school start in the ancient, Agrarian Age schedule we're still using in this day and age.

If I were to get to my office using a horse and buggy, people would look at me like I'm crazy and the police would likely order me off the road. But starting work at the same time as people did hundreds, and even thousands, of years ago? Nah, no problem! Go right ahead, sir!

This is the very definition of insanity. It's also largely at the root of why night owls suffer such high levels of discrimination in the workplace and elsewhere, when *we* should be ridiculing *them* for following such an ancient practice in modern times.

To make matters worse, we have to suffer with it quietly. I know I have. Night owls can't run and call some equal opportunity commission or have a civil rights lawyer take their case on contingency. No, we just have to take it, stuck in a world that's run to a large degree by early risers who believe that anyone who isn't one is somehow flawed or inferior.

Poorna Bell, writing in the *Huffington Post*, said that a friend once told her, "You can sleep when you're dead," then realized that if her friend continues to burn the candle at both ends as she always had, she would be the dead one sooner rather than later.

Perhaps "sleep when you're dead" is a self-fulfilling prophecy? The deleterious effects of elevated cortisol seem to indicate so, if nothing else does, but then again few things can be as harmful to your health as high cortisol.

Bell goes on to wonder why we persist in this ridiculous idea that existing on as little sleep as possible means you're somehow tougher or more resilient.

"Well, It's Nice of You to Join Us"

Of all the sleep-shaming sayings that the early birds love to use, few, perhaps none, are as insulting as this one. It's as if they're suggesting that we deliberately showed up last, as if we did it on purpose.

I can't even count how many times I've heard this saying over the years, and continue to hear it. Nowadays it's from well-meaning relatives who say it in a good-natured, humorous way, yet they're entirely unaware of how much it stings and brings me back to times and situations I'd rather forget about. If you're wondering why I don't bring up the fact that it's a very unpleasant thing to hear, I've tried. All it leads to is more sleep-shaming and asking what the big deal is about getting up earlier.

Most often it was when I was working for a moron of a sales manager who would insist on morning sales meetings. One complete idiot held them Mondays, Wednesdays, and Fridays at 8:00 a.m., and an even bigger idiot held them daily at 7:30 a.m.

As you might imagine, there was nothing much to talk about or discuss at those meetings. They were merely a power play on the unqualified sales managers' behalf, in order to get satisfaction from watching us comply with their orders.

If you think I'm joking about those managers being totally unqualified and on a power trip, I used to work with someone who was terrible at sales, or perhaps would have been if he'd actually tried. Instead he spent years job-hopping, always having the next position lined up, complete with start-up pay,* before being fired from the current one.

In any case, he finally got a sales manager job because the company wanted to get him out of sales but was a big dumb company that preferred to transfer people internally rather than fire them for nonperformance. And what did he do at that job?

You guessed it: He was one of those little dictator sales managers who made everyone come in for an early morning meeting and chronically micromanaged everyone until they got fed up and quit.

---

*In sales it's not uncommon for a company to pay a salesperson a bit extra for the first few months, or "start-up" pay, until he or she gets commissions coming in, which of course this particular person never did.

He took particular revenge on people who had wronged him in one way or another, or so he perceived, by putting them on warning and making them come to see him daily and show him that they'd met his minimum level of activity for the day.

Looking back, I can run through the various sales managers I had worked for over the years until striking out on my own, and all but two fit that description.

These guys were morons—I mean totally clueless—about sales. That's why they forced everyone to cold call all day, every day; they didn't know what else to do. They had no idea how to manage a sales team, let alone how to sell!

And it was this type of manager in particular, the low IQ idiot, who would most frequently sleep-shame and say things like, "It's nice of you to join us."

Remember in the previous chapter, about how chronically high cortisol levels in early risers make them grouchy and cranky? Maybe this is why those guys and gals were such total jerks, let alone clueless about performing their respective jobs?

Seriously now, I don't "morning-shame" early risers. Perhaps I do, a little, in this book, but that's because this is meant to be the night owl's manifesto, a jumping-off point, if you will, to making the most of your night owl tendencies and hopefully to help promote flexible work schedules and other solutions to accommodate night owls and quit discriminating against them.

After all, it's harmful to one's health to get up too early. Even natural early risers experience the negative health effects of early rising. Night owls who are forced to rise early not only have the health consequences to deal with, but also struggle even to survive on a morning work schedule.

Eating and breathing are obviously essential to survive, and so is sufficient sleep. But how are night owls supposed to get enough sleep to remain healthy if they cannot fall asleep before a certain time, then are forced back out of bed five or six hours later to get to a job they depend on? And if we do get enough sleep, we get fired (worst case) and sleep-shamed (best case, if you can even call that a best-case scenario).

The Very Real Effects of Sleep Deprivation on Your Health

Getting too little sleep has dire health consequences, yet it's a condition that night owls all too often find themselves living with—perpetually. The thing about night owls isn't so much that we can't get up early, more that we can't fall asleep early. And if one goes to bed late—something over which night owls have no real choice notwithstanding some as yet unknown medical breakthrough—one must get up late in order to get enough sleep.

But in the real world, if you want to make it through school, or if you want to keep that job, you must comply with their schedule. And for night owls that all too often means living with sleep deprivation.

Just what does sleep deprivation cause? It causes all kinds of health problems, and here are the primary ones:

Memory issues: During sleep your brain rests, recovers, and processes information. Lack of sleep negatively affects both short- and long-term memory. Think about the last time you were sleep deprived, and couldn't remember why you walked into a particular room.

Mood alterations: Moodiness, anxiety, depression, being overly emotional, and having a quick temper are all effects of insufficient sleep.

Difficulty concentrating: Concentration, cognitive ability, and problem thinking skills all suffer when you don't get enough sleep.

Automobile and other accidents: Fatigue resulting from inadequate sleep leads to more automobile and other accidents; this is further complicated by the aggression caused by caffeine and high cortisol levels.

Lowered immunity: Adequate sleep is a basic requirement for a robust immune system and a lack thereof leads to increased frequency and severity of colds, flu, and other infections.

Hypertension: Sleeping less than your body actually requires increases the risk of high blood pressure.

Heightened risk of diabetes: Insufficient sleep adversely affects your body's insulin response; insulin is the hormone responsible for regulating blood sugar levels and lack of adequate sleep can lead to type 2 diabetes.

Weight gain: Insufficient sleep throws off the balance of hormones and neurotransmitters that tell you if you are full or if you are hungry; without adequate sleep you're far more likely to overeat.

Cardiovascular disease: Sleep deprivation leads to high blood pressure, which in turn leads to other cardiovascular problems and heightened risk of heart disease.

Low sex drive: If you don't get enough sleep your sex drive will likely suffer. This leads to problems in marriage and other romantic/sexual relationships. In men specifically, inadequate sleep may reduce testosterone levels.

Poor balance: Lack of sleep negatively affects your balance and coordination, increasing your risk for injury.

Yikes! And to think the sleep-shamers are doing all of this to far too many night owls! Let's take a closer look at some issues in particular:

Difficulty Concentrating and Other Mental Dysfunctions

A 1997 National Sleep Foundation poll estimated that $1.8 billion in work productivity is lost due to fatigue in the workplace each year. (And that's in two-decades-ago dollars.) The American Chiropractic Association has said that memory, decision-making ability, attention, and patience are just a few of the limiting issues associated with insufficient sleep.

Imagine you bought a Ferrari, excited to finally drive at 200 mph, when your boss goes outside to the parking garage and puts a limiter on the car that caps the speed at 60 mph. You'd be furious. How dare your boss alter something that's entirely out of his or her authority at work? Yet that's what they're doing to you, around the clock, when they force you to be at work bright and early in the morning. (Don't you hate that "bright and early" cliché?) Forced early rising and the consequential sleep deprivation are the equivalent to putting such a limiter on your brain.

"Sleep Debt"

There's a myth in society that you can cut your sleep hours short all week and then somehow make up for it on weekends. The sad truth is that you cannot, and the research is there to prove it. It makes one wonder if the early rising sleep-shamers made this one up just so we'd get up earlier!

Negative Impact on Relationships

You already know that early risers tend to be grouchy and on edge all the time, thanks to elevated levels of the stress hormone cortisol. These same negative effects occur when you don't get enough sleep, and can severely impact your interpersonal relationships. Inadequate sleep makes you more irritable, and it leaves you in a haze, or a state of "brain fog," not allowing you to be fully present with your partner.

Patrick Finan, PhD, a sleep researcher at Johns Hopkins University, points out that insufficient sleep raises your obesity risk by 50%, can triple your risk of type 2 diabetes, and is tied to a 33% increase in your risk for dementia. So get enough sleep, dammit!

The One-Sided Story That Won't Go Away

In an article by Alyss Bowen on Grazia, entitled "Can We Please Stop Sleep Shaming Everyone?" she asks, "Can we just not?" Ironically, she's an early riser, but living in the UK, she's clearly more enlightened than Americans on this topic.

"What time did you wake up this morning? Was it at around 6 a.m. so you could put on your gym kit and head out the door to go on a casual 8.5 km run before your sleeping flatmates arose from their slumber? Or perhaps it was 30 minutes after your pre-set alarm, because you'd spent the past 30 minutes snoozing, clinging on to those last moments of sleep before you had to face the commute to work?"

She then goes on to wonder why there are 348 million Google results for "the top 7 benefits of waking up early," and "healthy reasons to be up early," when scientific and medical studies entirely contradict those myths. She was even concerned about not being quite "clever" enough herself after reading studies showing that night owls are both smarter and more creative!

Maybe enough early risers will ask the same kinds of questions and start making positive changes for the rest of us if we get enough copies of this book into their hands.

Bowen goes on to admit that while she's up, wired, and ready for the day at 6:45 a.m., she's yawning "enough for three people" come night.

In a separate article, Kate Hughes wonders why there's no water-shaming for people who get the recommended eight cups a day of water, yet society shames people for getting the recommended eight hours of sleep.

Enough is enough already.

Unintended Sleep-Shaming Is Everywhere

Headspace has been the app I've used in the past to attempt to learn to meditate, the key word here being *attempt*. Knowing that several more have come to market since Headspace debuted, I was checking out reviews and comparisons of various meditation apps when I saw this article in the sidebar: "The Ultimate Guide to Being a Morning Person."

Just when I was in a great mood, feeling productive, having just chatted with my doctor about which app he uses, I was slapped in the face with this bit of sleep-shaming.

Now don't get me wrong: I'm sure the author of this article is, first, a natural morning person—they're the only people who believe that anyone can become a morning person too—and second, that the author has been hammered from birth with the brainwashing and believes there's value in perpetuating it.

This is *not* what I wanted to stumble upon while seeking to better learn meditation and live life more mindfully!

Since this is a topic that obviously interests me, I read the article, and it was utter rubbish. The "advice" to become a morning person was to lay your clothes out the night before (duh), do squats while brushing your teeth (which can lead to injury or muscle strain in night owls), set an alarm for everything, right down to when you should get dressed (talk about adding needless stress to mornings), read your to-do list aloud while in the shower (seriously?), and while getting ready to head out the door, repeat aloud the things you need to bring, such as wallet, keys, phone, and so on.

In summary, this article had nothing of value that would help someone to get up earlier. Instead it was written by yet another self-serving morning person, who needed to come up with something to write about to fulfill her journalistic obligations for the day, and sadly chose to write an utterly useless article that does nothing other than sleep-shame those of us who don't get up before the sun.

One thing I'll grant the author is that she probably did not intend to sleep-shame the rest of us. She merely echoed her own daily routine, which seems needlessly rushed and stressful to me, and, of course, morning people *love* to read articles like this one to validate their own sleep habits. Why else would another author have pointed out that there are 348 million Google search results on why it's better to be an early riser, when virtually every bit of science on the subject contradicts all of it? It's because cheap journalism is about telling people what they want to hear, rather than what they need to hear, so that readers will rave about the author and post great reviews.

And the unintended consequence of all this, or at least I hope it's unintended, is to sleep-shame and make night owls feel inferior. As always, many will try to follow this advice and only hurt their success prospects in the long run and cause unnecessary health problems to boot.

Night Owls Are Tired of Being Discriminated Against

In an article on Vox.com by Brian Resnick in April 2018, he explained why forcing night owls to comply with a morning-centric schedule will lead to severe health problems and premature death, along with the fact that chronotypes are inborn and that night owls cannot simply just become morning people, topics we've already covered. (Lots of luck trying to explain that to the self-serving morning people who impose those schedules.)

In conclusion, he writes:

In 2016, when I first reported on the science of chronobiology, I spoke to several people with delayed sleep phase, a condition that puts people on the extreme end of the night-owl chronotype. These people have a hard time falling asleep before 2 or 3 a.m. and prefer to sleep until around noon. There's nothing wrong with their sleep other than that their schedules for it are shifted.

These late sleepers are tired of being judged for a behavior they cannot easily control. If they can't change their sleep patterns, maybe society should become more accepting of them. We tend to assume that late wakers are the partiers, the deadbeats, the ones who are so irresponsible they can't keep a basic schedule. The people I spoke to found these assumptions to be personally damaging.

We should follow common sense for a solution. *People should be able to sleep when their bodies demand it.* Considering the potential health impacts of ignoring our biological clocks, it seems harmless enough to try. [Emphasis mine]

Night Owls, Sleep-Shaming, and Depression

There are endless studies out there claiming that early risers are statistically happier, and to a large degree, they're right. However, much like how studies showing that early risers perform better at work and at school are flawed due to the fact that such studies heavily favor early risers, so are studies claiming early risers are happier. *They're statistically happier because they get to live life on their natural sleep schedules.* What those researchers are not willing to talk about is the fact that so many night owls are unhappy, not because they're night owls—you've seen why we're more relaxed than morning people—but rather, because of being forced to live a life of compliance with early morning schedules and the ensuing sleep deprivation and even depression that follow.

While I've never personally experienced depression, I spent years going through the cycle of drinking to excess at night in order to fall asleep, usually combined with some kind of sleep aid such as Unisom, followed by excessive amounts of caffeine in the morning to get going again. Because I'd been doing this for so long, I reached the point where I no longer experienced hangovers after downing an entire bottle of white wine or a few generous drams of whisky the night before; however, I was feeling the effects of misusing alcohol and drinking to excess.

Most people are aware that heavy drinkers are an irritable lot, and I was no exception. I was constantly grouchy, pessimistic, constantly complaining about everything…you name it. All of that because I couldn't fall asleep at a reasonable hour without the stuff and wanted to avoid the "Z-Drugs" such as Ambien, which are far, far more addictive than alcohol. On top of that, many users report feeling like a zombie the next day, which entirely defeats the purpose of taking a sleep aid; what's the point when you're just as tired and brain-fogged the next day as if you had a night of insomnia?

Bear with me for a moment while I explain why alcohol causes anxiety, a problem I eventually came face-to-face with: Alcohol causes relaxation and drowsiness by binding to the GABA (gamma-aminobutyric acid) receptors in the brain. This is also how the benzodiazepine drugs work, which include Xanax, Valium, Klonopin, and the infamous Rophonyl (commonly known as the date rape drug "roofie"), among many others.

The reason Xanax in particular is so extremely addictive—multitudes more are addicted to it than to opioids—is because it's one of the most powerful of the bunch, and also one of the shortest acting, if not the shortest acting. What happens to Xanax users is that they experience either severe anxiety or feel a panic attack coming on, and pop a pill in response. What that pill does, much like alcohol, is bind to the GABA receptors in the brain, and since GABA is the relaxation neurotransmitter, the user feels a deep sense of calm and relaxation in anywhere from five to 15 minutes; Xanax comes on strong and it comes on fast.

However, when the drug wears off after three to four hours, the anxiety comes back—but this time, it's even worse! The user then takes another…and another…and the cycle continues to repeat itself into a nasty downward spiral. That's why Xanax in particular can cause physical addiction in as little as two days, and yet it's the most prescribed drug in America. (Meanwhile the ill-intentioned DEA and both state and federal lawmakers are singularly obsessed with regulating opioid painkiller drugs despite the fact that Xanax is far more dangerous and is ruining far more lives.)

This is also where the myth that alcohol is a sugar comes from. There's a very misguided belief that the reason you wake up a few hours after passing out drunk is because the so-called sugar in alcohol jolts you awake. This is totally, completely incorrect. Ethanol, the kind of alcohol we drink, is an alcohol. Sugar, meanwhile, is sugar. Ethanol cannot be a sugar any more than a fat can be a carbohydrate. It's chemically impossible.

Anyway, what really happens when you drink too much and then can't sleep a few hours later is exactly what happens when Xanax wears off: The GABA receptors in the brain rebound to a high enough degree to offset the time that they were depressed, and…*boom*! You're wide awake!

One listed side effect of benzodiazepine drugs such as Xanax is that they can lead to depression. That's because artificially activated levels of GABA literally depress the rest of the brain. That's where the calmness and tranquility these drugs produce come from; however, over time they can make the user *permanently* depressed.

The same is true with alcohol, since it's also a "GABAergic" drug; in fact, alcohol is classified as a depressant! To put that in perspective, it does the opposite of what antidepressants do: Alcohol actually *causes* depression when used long-term.

And on that note, it's why night owls who use alcohol nightly, or any of the other mentioned drugs, including sleeping pills such as Ambien and Lunesta, which also work by activating GABA receptors in the brain, are highly prone to depression versus the rest of the population that doesn't struggle to get up early to get to work in time.

As to caffeine, it has a surprisingly long biological half-life. In plain English, that means it hangs around in your body much longer than you'd like to think it does. And what happens when we're not only trying to get to sleep hours earlier than our normal time, but are also still unknowingly wired by caffeine?

That's right, we go right back to using sleep aids, whether it happens to be a few Benadryl tablets or copious amounts of Scotch. And the endless cycle goes on and on, ad infinitum, ad nauseam, ad mortem. Night owls get stuck in a continuous cycle of poisoning themselves day and night, all to be able to cope with a morning work schedule. And it goes without saying that all of these various drugs—alcohol, caffeine, and others—negatively impact our cognitive ability and performance at work, making the prospect of promotions and pay raises all the more difficult to attain.

Nick Norton, who holds the very impressive triple-crown title of law student, yogi, and writer, wrote an article for *Huffington Post*, dated December 6, 2017, entitled "Diary of a Depressed Night Owl: The Search for Happiness Late into the Evening."

It was this paragraph in particular that really grabbed my attention: "In addition to having a higher probability of success behind them, early risers are also statistically more happy. In many ways, that makes sense. Night owls are more likely to have to rely on sleeping pills or alcohol to go to sleep and caffeine to wake them up. When awake late into the night, I'm probably stressing about having to go to work or school the following morning. Even waking up late on a day off can be depressing because a whole day feels wasted."

So it's not just alcohol, caffeine, benzos, and other drugs that can lead to depression in night owls who are forced to fight their inner clock. It's also the experience of insomnia and lying awake all night, consumed with anxiety over having to wake so early. And his comment about feeling depressed over waking up late on a day off? There's nothing wrong with that; it's society's sleep-shaming and constant denigration of night owls that causes such guilt.

As Mr. Burns in *The Simpsons* said so well, "A happy worker is a productive worker." When employers finally take heed and allow their night owl employees to be happy, things will be better for everyone all around.

As a fitting conclusion to this chapter, I'd like to point out that while Xanax may be the single most prescribed drug in America, antidepressants are the most prescribed class of drugs. Like Xanax, they're nothing to mess around with or take lightly, and one must wonder if the explosion in antidepressant prescriptions in recent years is directly connected to the fact that forced early rising frequently leads to depression in night owls.

Antidepressant drugs are just as addictive—I've watched a relative go through a living hell trying to get off one after taking it for only one week. That one week turned into *three months* of slowly tapering off the drug in order to avoid severe withdrawals. And if that's not enough to give you pause, consider the fact that all but one mass shooter in the past 50 years were taking antidepressants, and that recently unsealed medical records of Frank Sinatra revealed that he passed away due to complications of taking an antidepressant and not from natural causes. Think about that.

Morning Madness

Our society harshly penalizes those who discriminate against people of different races, sexual identity, religion, and rightly so, yet the very real existence of discrimination against night people is widely accepted by society despite the very real and severe dangers to the health of night people who are forced to rise with the early birds. This is another example of the tyranny of the majority, something that African Americans, LGBTQ people, and many other groups managed to combat through endless hard work, vigilance, and, most of all, a simple refusal to tolerate further discrimination. The time has come for night owls to band together and do the same. Discrimination is discrimination regardless of whom it's being committed against, and it's always wrong regardless of which group is being targeted.

13

Diet, Nutrition, and Other Secrets to Better, Deeper Sleep

Early to rise and early to bed makes a man healthy and wealthy and dead.

—James Thurber

DISCLAIMER: The information presented from hereon in is based on my own personal experience along with thousands of hours of research. I am *not* a doctor and don't pretend to be one, so it's essential that you check with your healthcare provider prior to using any dietary supplements or any other advice given.

It's obvious that the so-called "problem" with us night owls is not so much that we can't get up early, but the fact that we have difficulty falling asleep at what society deems to be a reasonable hour.

I've personally struggled with this all my life, or at least until I started the business that set me free from society's dictates; now that I have kids, I struggle with it once again because I like to see them—and my beautiful wife—before they head out the door in the mornings. And considering the fact that they leave at 7:40 a.m., that's really, really early for me!

Having said that, on days when I do manage to get up around 7:30 a.m. and see them, I realize the full advantage of being a night owl. That's because even though my rising time is earlier than my internal clock dictates, the beautiful truth is that night owls can go the distance while early risers cannot! So, while I may have gotten up two hours later than they did—still early by my standards!—I can keep on going and going long after they've crashed and called it quits for the day.

On those days I take my time waking up and getting ready, knowing that I have the house to myself for a while. Then I head out to my office, where I'm extremely productive since we night owls don't crash and burn in the early- to mid-afternoon the way early birds do. In fact it's not uncommon for me to have one of those days when I awaken early, or early for me anyway, only to really get in the zone as far as work goes and head home well past 7:00 p.m.

So, whether you have a reason to want to get up a bit earlier than your natural rhythm would like, which in my case is the desire to see my family before they all leave, or if you're forced to get up early for work or school—which is most often the case—the million-dollar question is, how to get to sleep at a decent hour?

I struggle with this. Even today as I write this, I can think back to last night and how completely wired I was around ten or eleven o'clock. Thankfully I've come up with an evening/night-time routine that allows me to get my shut-eye earlier than usual when the need arises.

A Look at Drug-Based Sleep Aids

I personally do not recommend pharmaceutical sleep aids for a variety of reasons. Here are some of the most common medications that are prescribed for insomnia.

The "Z-Drugs"

If you're ever had a prescription for sleeping pills, you've taken one of the Z-Drugs. This class of drugs gets their nickname from the generic/chemical names of the drugs; for example, generic Ambien is called zolpidem, and so on.

Remember the discussion about the highly addictive class of drugs known as the benzodiazepines? They include tranquilizers such as Xanax, Valium, Ativan, and many others. These drugs work very similarly to alcohol in that they bind to the GABA—gamma-aminobutyric acid—receptors in the brain. GABA is the "calming" neurotransmitter. It is the chief inhibitory compound in the human body.

However, as seen, these drugs have a strong rebound effect. In fact, the reason Xanax is perhaps the most addictive prescription drug out there, known to cause addiction in as little as two days, is that it quashes panic and anxiety for 3–4 hours, but then it all comes back—even stronger! This causes the patient to take more and more and more, until either a stronger drug or a higher dose is needed. Over time these drugs can cause cognitive impairment. Stevie Nicks, of Fleetwood Mac fame, said that the benzodiazepine drug clonazepam, brand-name Klonopin, stole her life and years of memories from her. That is just how dramatic and far-reaching the negative effects of these drugs can be with long-term use.

Similarly, the Z-Drugs also bind to the brain's GABA receptors at the same location as the benzodiazepines. They act slightly differently in that their intended purpose is to cause drowsiness and to induce sleep, while the benzodiazepines are intended to reduce anxiety; however, anyone who has taken any of the benzos will tell you how sedating they are, particularly the stronger ones such as Xanax (alprazolam).

The problem, then, should be obvious: Since these drugs work on the same brain receptors, at the same locations, as the benzodiazepines, they are equally as addictive and dangerous when used any longer than the month or so that experts agree on as the maximum length of time to depend upon these drugs for sleep.

Someone who I know personally had bouts of intermittent insomnia and finally went to see his physician to do something about it. He was prescribed Ambien, which he said, "Knocked me on my ass," and he slept great. For two weeks.

Then he decided he was sleeping well again and that he didn't need the Ambien.

Didn't need it? He was hooked! He recounted the sheer hell of not sleeping at all for an entire week just to get off the pills. And he took them for only two weeks, and at less than the prescribed dosage, to boot.

Another big problem with these drugs is that they are Schedule IV controlled substances in the United States. As mentioned earlier in reference to the "opioid epidemic," more and more physicians are refraining from prescribing controlled substances out of fear of being subjected to a DEA review, which for a doctor is roughly equivalent to being subjected to an IRS audit for me or you.

That means your doctor may simply decline to renew your prescription one day, and—BOOM! You're going to be lying awake for a week straight or longer as my friend did. Finally, since these drugs work very similarly to both alcohol and the benzodiazepines, they also carry the same withdrawal symptoms:

tremor, seizures, delirium tremens, and so on, are all potential risks with abrupt cessation of any of the Z-Drugs.

More "Z-Drug" Zingers

Another sticking point I have with the Z-Drugs, aside from the fact that they're a chemical assistant and not a natural way to get to sleep, is the bizarre behavior they commonly induce, including amnesia, sleep-walking, sleep-eating, sleep-sex, and yes, even sleep-driving!

In one extreme case, a man who was taking Ambien for sleep got up at night, retrieved a firearm, and committed a mass shooting in his sleep. He went home and went back to bed with no memory of the event. Subsequent interrogations and polygraph examinations confirmed that the man truly did not remember the horrific things he did that night.

Sleep-induced shootings aside, just the thought of sleep-driving is terrifying to me, especially when I know that it could happen without my knowledge and that I could easily get myself, and others, killed by doing it.

For these and many more reasons, I consider the Z-Drugs like Ambien and Lunesta to be of questionable safety and efficacy.

Antidepressants

As newer and better antidepressants hit the market, older ones are relegated to taking up the slack in other departments. Most notable is the prescription antidepressant trazodone, which, believe it or not, is now the number one most prescribed drug to treat insomnia in the United States.

Similar drugs are sometimes prescribed, albeit off-label, for help with falling asleep. For example, the muscle relaxant cyclobenzaprine, brand-name Flexeril, is actually a slightly modified tricyclic antidepressant known for its drowsiness-inducing effects.

My concern here is, once again, that the drug is acting as a band-aid rather than naturally inducing restful sleep. Furthermore, the implications of prescribing antidepressants to people who are not clinically depressed and therefore don't need them are still highly questionable. There are the usual side effects of antidepressants such as loss of libido, and in the case of tricyclics or muscle relaxants, severe dry mouth that leads to tooth erosion and cavities.

Antihistamines

Who hasn't ever taken NyQuil and then sung the praises of how great they slept afterward?

NyQuil puts you to sleep through the use of an antihistamine, doxylamine, which is very similar to how Benadryl (generic name diphenhydramine) works. Seemingly everyone knows that Benadryl will cause drowsiness and works great as a sleep aid. I know I've used both doxylamine and diphenhydramine myself on and off over the years. (After surgery I used them to sleep, since opioid painkillers give me pretty severe insomnia.)

The main problem with these types of drugs, other than the fact that they leave many people feeling groggy and like "zombies" the next morning, is that they block the all-important neurotransmitter acetylcholine in the brain. It is the neurotransmitter released by the nervous system in order to activate muscles. That means effects can range from the mild and unnoticeable to the severe, up to and including seizures and paralysis. It's also a neurotransmitter in the sympathetic nervous system and as the final product released by the parasympathetic nervous system.

The brain contains several cholinergic areas that rely on acetylcholine, including influencing functions such as arousal, attention, memory, and motivation.

Most people take these drugs in the form of over-the-counter allergy meds such as Claritin and Zyrtec, which are low dose and pose little problem, although long-term consequences still exist.

At the University of Washington's School of Pharmacy, a team led by pharmacist Shelley Gray tracked approximately 3,500 people aged 65 or older. Using the group's pharmacy records to determine all drugs each participant had taken over the past 10 years up to the study, it was found that the approximately 800 people who had developed dementia within another 10 years were taking anticholinergic drugs. What's more, the study found that taking an anticholinergic for three years or more was associated with a whopping 54% increase in dementia risk versus taking the same dose for three months or less.

For these reasons I do not stand by the use of antihistamines/anticholinergics like Benadryl and Unisom. When I happen to take Zyrtec or another allergy medication during the times of year when my allergies sometimes act up, I make a point to take a choline supplement with breakfast in order to counter the choline-reducing effects in order to hopefully prevent the long-term consequences of taking this class of drugs.

Natural and Herbal Sleep Aids

Nope, by herbal I do not mean marijuana, so don't get your hopes up! Instead, here are some of the most common herbal sleep aids available as over-the-counter supplements, including ones I've used.

Valerian Root

If you've ever taken valerian root, you'll remember it: The stuff stinks like days-old moldy gym socks and you'd better have water at the ready because hunting for it with that capsule in your mouth is no walk in the park!

Valerian root has been shown to reduce the amount of time to fall asleep by 15–20 minutes. It also helps to improve sleep quality. Recommended dosages are between 400 and 900 mg, taken two hours prior to bedtime, although I find that I sleep through the night better if I take it right at bedtime.

While valerian doesn't work as quickly or effectively as sleeping pills such as the Z-Drugs, it's a safe alternative, and what's more, it can help with the insomnia and other withdrawal symptoms when coming off a Z-Drug.

Passionflower

Passionflower is commonly used for a variety of ailments, the most common of which are insomnia and anxiety.

On the anxiety front, passionflower has been shown in some clinical trials to be as effective as some of the benzodiazepines in reducing anxiety when taken twice daily. Unlike valerian, while it's calming, it won't knock you on your ass, although you should experiment on a weekend or other free day first to see how it affects you before getting behind the wheel.

It is also useful for preoperative anxiety when taken 30–90 minutes before rolling into the operating room.

As for sleep, there isn't much research on this topic as there is anecdotal evidence, such as my personal experiences. Having said that, early research shows that passionflower tea taken an hour before bedtime for seven consecutive nights improves subjective ratings of sleep quality. Research also shows that taking a product containing passionflower, valerian, and hops (NSF-3 by M/s Tablets in India) for two weeks improves sleep similar to zolpidem (Ambien) in people with insomnia.

Kava

There is a lot of controversy over kava regarding liver health; in fact, it's been banned in both Europe and Canada for this reason. However, research shows that it was a particular, single brand of kava that contained extracts from the entire plant, rather than just the root, that led to the hepatoxicity and cases of liver failure.

Having taken the herb for years and having gotten regular annual labs done by my doctor, I can tell you with certainty that my liver function values weren't even slightly elevated, ever. However, my disclaimer still stands, and you should do your own research and/or consult with a healthcare professional prior to taking kava.

Kava has been proven effective in the treatment of anxiety, which is not surprising considering the fact that medications and supplements with antianxiety properties also cause some degree of drowsiness, which is why many un- or underinformed physicians will prescribe benzos such as Xanax off-label for sleep. (The practice of prescribing something off-label refers to prescribing a drug for a purpose outside the scope of its FDA approval, which is entirely legal; doctors have discretion here.)

Studies show that taking kava extracts that contain 70% kavalactones, something you should look for on labels before buying, reduce anxiety, sometimes to the same degree that prescription antianxiety medications do. However, this can take up to five weeks of daily use to take full effect and doesn't provide immediate relief like the benzos do.

On that same note, it has been shown that slowly increasing the dose of kava over one week while simultaneously reducing the dose of a benzo over the course of two weeks can prevent most withdrawal symptoms and avoid severe rebound anxiety in patients coming off benzodiazepine drugs. Remember that they have some of the highest addiction potential as well as the most dangerous withdrawals of nearly any class of drugs. This is important to remember if you've struggled with quitting these drugs in the past but simply keep refilling your prescription because you've found it impossible to withdraw.

On the sleep front, which is why we're here, some research shows that taking a kava extract daily for four weeks reduces sleeping problems, while other research contradicts this and states that it only reduces anxiety, not insomnia.

Knowing from personal experience that anxiety and anxiety alone can cause severe insomnia due to the endless thoughts in your head, the racing heartbeat, and so on, I see a strong connection between medications and supplements that control anxiety and the treatment of insomnia. Remember, the most common antianxiety drugs, the benzodiazepines, cause drowsiness, are commonly prescribed for sleep, and are nearly chemically identical to the Z-Drugs, which all support this hypothesis that antianxiety treatments work well for sleep.

Magnesium

Commonly known as a metal and an essential mineral in the human body, magnesium is a calming mineral that is known for its ability to reduce blood pressure, relieve stress, and improve sleep quality and prevent insomnia.

Magnesium works on helping you sleep by helping to regulate both melatonin, the sleep hormone, as well as several brain neurotransmitters. Research shows that there is a correlation between magnesium and melatonin levels in the body. Magnesium-deficient individuals commonly report insomnia and reduced sleep quality. Additional research shows that magnesium is tied to your circadian rhythm.

Magnesium promotes relaxation and assists with sleep by binding to GABA receptors, just like several prescription drugs previously discussed. This binding activity slows down nervous system activity, which calms you and your body overall and prepares you for slumber.

Sleep is just one small facet of magnesium's myriad benefits; hence why it's considered an essential mineral. It's also known to be a muscle relaxant, and some studies show that magnesium glycinate, 400 mg taken twice daily, is just as effective as prescription muscle relaxants such as Skelaxin. I personally take the glycinate salt of magnesium over other varieties primarily because, unlike other varieties, it does not have any laxative properties, and is very well-absorbed by the body. (Magnesium oxide, the most commonly store-bought form of magnesium, is also the cheapest to manufacture and is very poorly absorbed; hence why it's found in many lower-cost multivitamins. Magnesium citrate is used specifically as a laxative, hence why I avoid it.)

One thing to absolutely avoid are "cal-mag" supplements, those containing both calcium and magnesium. While both are essential minerals, the issue is that the two are antagonistic to each other, meaning that taking both at the same time means neither will have its intended effect. It is best, therefore, to take calcium, if you take it at all, in the morning, and to take magnesium with your evening meal and possibly at bedtime as well. Some nutritional experts even go so far as recommending that you take them on entirely separate days, alternating back and forth.

I do not take calcium supplements at all, first because it's an excitatory mineral and my mind is very active as it is without the need for any additional stimulation, and second, and perhaps more important, because so much of what we consume, right down to bottled water, is overcalcified and has caused something of a magnesium deficiency epidemic in our society. In other words, calcium is everywhere in foods and beverages you consume, but not so much with magnesium.

Finally, if you consume alcohol regularly, it's especially imperative that you supplement with magnesium. Alcohol consumption drastically depletes magnesium levels in the body, requiring replacement with a supplement. Those who have had gastric bypass or other GI surgery that affects absorption of nutrients should also be on the lookout for magnesium deficiency symptoms such as anxiety and insomnia.

Melatonin

Melatonin, contrary to popular belief, is neither an herb nor a supplement; it is a hormone that's naturally produced in the human body via serotonin, magnesium, and other chemicals in the body. (That's why many SSRI antidepressants, that act solely by increasing serotonin levels in the brain, also cause drowsiness as a side effect.)

Melatonin is also perhaps the most misused of sleep aids due to the fact that it's sold in tablet form at supraphysiological dosages, or in plain English, much, much more than is necessary or even desirable to take.

On a recent trip to my local pharmacy I was looking for 0.3 mg melatonin tablets, or 300 mcg. No luck! The lowest dose I could find was 3 mg, or 10 times the dose I was seeking. They even had 10 mg tablets in the store! And yet, nothing remotely near safe and recommended doses.

Your body's melatonin production is regulated entirely by light. It's a big reason that night owls are night owls; due to our innate circadian rhythms, our bodies begin to produce melatonin later and also stop producing it later. That's why we fall asleep late and get up late. During winter when the days are short, or during dreary days in general, much of the sluggishness experienced by people comes from the lack of adequate sunlight needed to shut off melatonin production. This is why sleep therapy lights are so effective for waking up, and to some degree, even shifting your rhythm and wake time, although we've seen that it's not possible to make any drastic changes there. You have what you were born with, and only small changes are possible, say, getting up one hour earlier. Maximum.

Likewise, melatonin is the reason why light can keep so many of us awake, particularly night owls. I use blackout curtains in my bedroom and make sure any light sources, for example, the power light on my air purifier, are covered up with black tape. I don't recommend the wake-up strategy of leaving your curtains and blinds open so the sunlight can come in and wake you in the morning, due to the fact that even trace amounts of light coming in can mess with your sleep. This is particularly true when there's a full moon, or when it's overcast out and urban light is reflecting back down.

Start with taking 0.3 mg, or 300 mcg, about two hours before bedtime. A common mistake people make is to take it at bedtime; however, the body naturally begins to produce it after dark or once you're home for the night under artificial lighting.

If you have the problem of waking frequently through the night, sublingual melatonin supplements are available that are absorbed instantly into the bloodstream when allowed to melt under your tongue, getting you back to sleep very quickly. Another option is time-release melatonin, commonly available in stores, if you're someone who wakes frequently throughout the night.

Check with your doctor or pharmacist, or use an online drug interaction checker, to make sure melatonin won't interfere with anything else you're taking. In particular, anticlotting drugs such as Warfarin, immunosuppressants such as corticosteroids (prednisone), diabetes drugs, and birth control pills can cause interactions with melatonin.

Finally, despite cautioning you on using too much melatonin, it is a very powerful antioxidant and is very good for your overall health. However, that doesn't necessarily mean that more is better, unless you want to feel like a zombie in the morning!

Good Sleep Hygiene

Myriad books, articles, and what-have-you have been written on the importance of so-called sleep hygiene, and I'll give you the run-down here, especially what works well for me, a night owl.

Proper Lighting

As mentioned, even low amounts of stray light can keep a night owl awake for hours. That's why it's so important to make sure you do what needs to be done to control nighttime light in your bedroom.

I use blackout curtains and also close the blinds behind them, while blacking out any power buttons or other extraneous electronic light sources. My clock has very dim red lighting, which I keep so dim I can barely read the clock when I wake up and am still in that blurry and groggy state of having just awakened.

Sleep masks are recommended and you should try it out and see what works best for you. I used them for a long time and then stopped, because of two reasons. One, having something on my head all night was enough to give me sleep problems and frequently wake me up, despite spending a small fortune on a super soft and comfortable sleep mask. Second, I frequently found myself waking up way, way too late with a sleep mask on. Even with the blackout curtains, I can still tell when it's daylight out, and will check the clock; as long as it's not six or some other crazy hour, I get up. With the sleep mask I would routinely wake up as much as two hours past my usual rising time, and on top of that, the unnecessary extra sleep would leave me feeling so groggy and brain-fogged that I would've been better off just fighting through a toss-and-turn night! Hence why I suggest that you try it out and see if it works for you or not.

Finally, if you must keep a smartphone on your nightstand, make sure it's on airplane mode and do-not-disturb, unless you're on call for work. Also use a feature such as Night Shift on iPhone or one of the apps that can dim your backlight and remove the blue light element from it (more on that later), and keep the phone's brightness at the minimum level.

Proper Sound

You're probably guessing that I'm going to recommend total and complete silence; however, that's the polar opposite of how I sleep, and once again, you'll have to try it both ways and find out what works best for you.

Personally I have trouble sleeping in a quiet room because I have exceptional hearing—I don't understand why, after playing in rock bands and sitting in the front row at dozens of concerts—but I do. I hear everything in the house, and my wife even marveled about this one time long ago when we were still dating. She was on the opposite side of the house, with the air conditioner running loudly (it was an older house in Phoenix), my noise generator was on in my room, the door was closed, and she was on the phone at a distance that should have been way out of earshot for me.

When I got up, I said, "So, Frank will do...," which was a comment on her phone call. And she was taken aback! So, yes, my seemingly supernatural hearing ability makes it tough for me to sleep in total silence.

What I do is twofold. First, I have an air purifier, as mentioned previously. It's big and it's loud, and that's how I like it—it blocks out any other sound I might possibly hear other than my Great Dane's very loud bark. Second, I've used a noise generator on and off. In the past you had to buy one, but now there are endless free noise generator apps you can get on your smartphone. Just remember to follow my advice about smartphones on your nightstand if you go this route.

If silence works for you, then perhaps heavier drapes and even acoustic foam in the right spots will really deaden it for you. You may also want to try earplugs, something I use particularly on weekends when the kids will have been up for a couple of hours by the time I get up, and of course the big dog usually manages to bark at something! I haven't found any one particular brand or variety of earplugs to be any more comfortable than others—or very much comfortable at all for that matter—so I simply use the inexpensive ones that I keep in my range bag, that I carry to the shooting range and competitions.

Foam earplugs are disposable, so dispose of them after one or two uses, otherwise you run the risk of ear infections due to mold, fungus, and bacteria. On the same note, if you are prone to ear infections at all, your ears need to breathe, so avoid them entirely.

Proper Temperature

This is one of the biggest mistakes people make: keeping their houses and/or bedrooms entirely too warm for deep, restful sleep.

It happens to me all the time when I travel, so much so that I've gotten to the point of drop-shipping a cheap tabletop fan from Amazon to the hotel ahead of time; that way I don't have to go hunting around for one, and I know which cheapie ones work well. Considering that they're under $20 and most hotels charge a daily, bogus "resort fee" of at least $25, apparently for the "free" wifi, I see it as a cheap investment in good sleep, whether the trip is for business or for pleasure. And heck, I'm sure at least a few members of hotel housekeeping staff have appreciated the free fan to take home!

The best temperature for falling asleep is in the low- to mid-60s. Most people consider this "cold" but this is the body's natural sleep temperature. Maintaining proper temperature helps ensure that your body will properly thermoregulate during sleep.

I've found about 65 degrees Fahrenheit to be ideal. Any lower than that and getting up in the middle of the night can be uncomfortably cold, and any warmer than that and I find myself hot, sweating, and tossing and turning all night. Remember, if it's too chilly, you can fix that with blankets, but too hot is too hot and there's nothing you can do about it other than lowering the thermostat.

I also like air moving around me. That means a ceiling fan, and, in summer months, a small table fan, like the one I use in hotels, aimed indirectly at the bed. Few things will keep you up all night like a fan blasting air directly at your face, so keep it indirect. Even when it's cool enough, if the air is stagnant, that can be enough to keep me needlessly awake. And remember, while some of these recommendations go well above and beyond the usual sleep hygiene recommendations, I'm one of your fellow night owls who struggles with getting and staying asleep and these extra measures will be necessary for us more often than not.

On a side note, if you're worried about the cost of things, such as natural sleep aids, blackout curtains, sleep masks, fans, and all that—not to mention a slightly higher electric bill thanks to the air conditioner—think of the cost that lost productivity does to you when you don't sleep well. It's not only financially damaging in terms of job or business performance; it also takes a toll on your well-being and overall happiness. So just make the investments needed to get a good night's sleep!

Avoid "Blue" Light at Night

By blue light, I'm referring to the light emitted by LCD and LED screens, found on everything from smartphones to tablets to computers to Apple Watches to your television to you-name-it. LED lightbulbs that emit a daytime light frequency, which most do, also fall under this category.

If you doubt the validity of this, open your smartphone, put it on the floor, walk to the other side of the room, and turn off the lights. Obviously this is best done at night. What you'll see is a big blast of blue light emanating from that screen!

The reason why electronics light can keep you awake is because it's the same light frequency as, well, daylight. Regular daylight on a sunny day, thanks to our blue sky, is not white light but actually a bluish hue, right around a light temperature of 5600 Kelvin. That's why photographers, when wanting to augment outdoor lighting, or do an indoor scene that simulates the outdoors, will set their lights to 5600 K. On the other end of the scale, for softer and/or "late" lighting, they'll drop way down to 2600 K to get that soft, yellowish hue.

The most common advice you'll hear is to avoid all screens for one to two hours prior to bedtime. However, this is more easily said than done in today's world.

I do agree with stopping work about an hour before bed, since it's the work itself, and not the light from the computer screen, that will keep my mind overflowing with thoughts and therefore keep me awake. When I do use a laptop at night, I use both the Night Shift feature along with the free f.lux app to remove the element of blue light. Using both together produces a very noticeable yellow light, which looks unnatural, but I value my sleep more than how good my computer screen looks! I also have a thin, blue-blocking screen protector film on the laptop. Unlike the apps, it doesn't look too far off from the natural screen light.

The same goes on tablets and phones—use blue-light reducing features such as Night Shift, apps that can do the same, and screen protector films that are hued to block some degree of blue light.

Since my wife and I have our handful of television shows we watch together, and there's no Night Shift on the TV (yet), I use a pair of cheap blue-blocking glasses I got on Amazon for under $20. If you're in your mid-forties like me and starting to use reading glasses, you can get over-the-counter reading glasses with the same blue-blocking tint. They do add some amount of yellowish tint to what you see, but once again, sleep quality is first and foremost with me and thus is far more important than any inconvenience it adds; having said that, I had to switch my Kindle highlights from yellow to blue because the yellow tint of the glasses combined with the yellowish light with the device turned to night mode was blocking them out completely to the point where I couldn't see the highlights!

Also, do not look at screens if you happen to wake up at night. This is especially important nowadays with seemingly everyone using his or her phones as nighttime clocks. Don't look at it. In fact, hide the clock altogether. Nothing is going to give you sleep anxiety and keep you awake more than seeing that you have to get up in two hours but feel like you need at least that much more sleep. It will merely cause you to lie awake thinking and worrying about it, guaranteeing that you indeed will not fall back asleep.

Avoid Daytime Naps

Unless you literally didn't sleep the previous night and absolutely require a nap to make it through the day, avoid napping. Even though it's so common, and many people swear by it, the fact is that napping is considered to be a symptom of a sleep disorder by medical science.

I for one cannot take the 20-minute "catnaps" people rave about and instead will fall into a regular, full 90-minute sleep cycle. This leaves me groggy for the rest of the day and feeling far more tired and sluggish than simply dealing with insomnia would have, so for me they're not worth it.

The more insidious part, however, is that daytime napping will interfere with your falling asleep and simply lead to more insomnia. It's like how Xanax rebounds and, after it wears off, the original anxiety is back—and it's worse!—and the user must take more frequent doses, and eventually higher doses, in order to get the same effect. Likewise, daytime napping can turn into rebound insomnia when you do try to get to bed on time, which leads to more insomnia, which leads to more napping, and you end up in the same vicious cycle as a Xanax addict.

So, in summary, no napping. Fight through the fatigue and save it for a great night's sleep!

Get Daytime Exercise

Many years ago I was experiencing insomnia and asked my then-doctor for sleeping pills. He said he will not prescribe them, and explains to patients that insomnia is more often than not due to lack of exercise and a sedentary lifestyle.

Think about it: If your body doesn't get enough exercise, it's never tired out and of course falling asleep will be a challenge! I got my ass back in gear, got back to pumping iron at the gym, and, amazingly, I almost immediately began sleeping *much* better!

One caveat, though, is to avoid exercise close to bedtime. Some light stretching as part of a nighttime routine is fine, but don't lift weights or do cardio or anything else that's going to elevate your heart rate and your body temperature with it. Remember the importance of keeping yourself cool in order to sleep well? If you do any kind of exercise that warms you up within three to four hours prior to bedtime, your body simply won't want to shut down for the night. The same goes for any kind of heavy lifting or any other strenuous activity. If the furniture needs rearranging, save it for the next day.

Get Daytime Sunshine!

This one sounds counterintuitive, so bear with me here.

You now know that your circadian rhythm, and the production and subsequent cessation of production of melatonin, are strongly tied to light. One of the issues night owls experience is that society demands we get up at a time when our rhythm is still stuck in the sleep phase and our bodies are producing melatonin. Hence why gloomy days and seasonal affective disorder can be especially problematic for night owls.

While I say "sunshine," what I really mean is any kind of daylight. Even many overcast, gloomy mornings will produce more natural outdoor light intensity than any therapy light can. It's important to get this light as soon as possible upon rising. It serves to terminate melatonin production, which gives you a boost in energy. It also stimulates vitamin D and serotonin production, both of which are feel-good neurotransmitters (well, vitamin D is a hormone, specifically a secosteroid and not a neurotransmitter, but it works to make you feel good and happy, simulate growth hormone production, and in men, stimulate testosterone production).

One myth about vitamin D is that you can get it from a supplement, and while true in theory, it is not the same substance that your body photosynthesizes during exposure to daylight. The vitamin D3 in pill bottles is called cholecalciferol, while the substance produced by your body is cholecalciferol sulfate. It's the naturally produced, sulfated version that has far-reaching and superior effects to the bottled version.

Just like the lipid hypothesis has been disproven and it's now known to medical science that cholesterol is not responsible for clogged and hardened arteries, it's also known that sun exposure in moderation, along with UVB-only* tanning beds in moderation, increases natural production of vitamin D3 which in turn prevents a myriad of health problems. Most interestingly, it's now known to prevent melanoma, the deadly form of skin cancer, which was previously blamed on sun exposure despite it most commonly appearing on areas such as the inner thighs and buttocks, which ordinarily get zero sun exposure.

While the FDA's daily recommended intake of vitamin D3 is well below what's now known to be beneficial, and irrelevant anyway if you're getting the natural form, it's important to know that you can accumulate too much D3 in your body, which can lead to toxicity. Also, because it assists with calcium absorption, you may be well-advised to avoid calcium supplements along with calcium-based antacids like Tums and Rolaids.

To really know where you're at, request a D3 check from your doctor or from a walk-in lab. Knowing what your levels are is the right start for getting them ideal. Also, I strongly recommend the book *The Vitamin D Cure* by James Dowd, MD (Wiley, 2012), to educate yourself on the importance of sunshine, not only for good sleep but for overall health. It does a great job of destroying the myths about skin cancer and other needless

---

*A note on UVB-only tanning beds: Although these beds are generally considered safe with moderate use, such as five minutes twice a week, they can be hard to find due to the fact that they don't produce much of a tan, if any at all. Tanning and burning come from UVA rays, while UVB rays in particular will stimulate D3 synthesis. Call around before going to a tanning salon to make sure they have these beds, and if you're in any doubt, consult with a healthcare professional and/or check out the book I just recommended.

mythology about sun exposure that has led to a D3-deficient nation and the long parade of health problems and illnesses that the deficiency causes.

Wake Up with a Therapy Light

I've mentioned therapy lights (or therapy lamps) earlier in the book and want to touch on them again here.

As with daylight, getting bright light as soon as you awaken, or are forced to wake up whatever the case may be, terminates your body's melatonin production so you can fully wake up and become alert and ready for the day.

The reason I like using a therapy light is convenience: I wake up, turn on the light and set it to the 30-minute timer, and sit up and read in bed until the light turns off. Then I'm wide awake and get up. It's more practical than getting up and trying to immediately get outside, particularly if the weather isn't inviting, or if you live somewhere like Seattle where even normal outdoor light levels can fall below those of a good, bright therapy light.

By shutting off melatonin production as soon as you wake up, you sort of "program" your body to turn it off at that same time every day. In turn, your body will begin to produce it a bit earlier in the evening, allowing you get to bed on time and fall asleep much more easily.

If you need to get up and move immediately and can't sit next to a therapy light for a half hour, another option is a light therapy visor. These will run you a lot more money—most go for over $100 or more—however, you can get your light exposure while "on the move" whether that's making coffee, eating breakfast, or whatever your morning routine entails.

On rainy days, which happen in Dallas a lot more than I'd care for, I'll bring my light out with me and plug it in on the kitchen counter while out there, and on the bathroom counter while getting ready. I know I can just get a visor, but until the light breaks, why bother?

TIP: Unplug your therapy light at night! I once dropped a tissue or something at night, and when I accidentally hit the power button on the light. *bam*—10,000 lux of 5600 K daylight right in my eyes! Thankfully I instantly clamped my eyes shut and took a sublingual melatonin and got back to sleep, but that was too close a call. Since the buttons are so light as to be practically touch-sensitive, I now unplug the light when not in use.

ANOTHER TIP: Sleep Cycle, the most popular sleep app out there, now integrates with Philips Hue lighting. I picked up four of their bulbs for my bedroom, synced them up with our wifi, and can now have the Sleep Cycle app gradually turn on the lights over a 30-minute period prior to my set waking time. This simulates the natural sunrise our bodies evolved to wake up to over millions of years. Better still, I can control the light temperature with the Hue app, ensuring a nice, bluish daylight hue to wake me up! Likewise, I can turn them way down or even change color, say to dark red, for nighttime use without interfering with melatonin and sleep.

Always Go to Bed at the Same Time (Optional)

This is a classic, time-tested piece of sleep hygiene advice, and it works—on most people.

During the week I go to bed when my body is naturally tired, with the help of some of the herbal sleep aids I mentioned. However, as a night owl, I love—and I mean love—staying up late. That is why I don't go to bed at the same time every night, and seriously question whether any true night owl can pull that one off.

The thing is, if I know I have something lined up the next morning, or a busy day in general, I'll pay attention to what time

I go to bed and sometimes will go easy on any sleep aids to avoid next-day grogginess.

However, if I have nothing planned the next day, other than the self-employed daily routine of figuring out what needs to be done next, I let my inner night owl come out to party and enjoy it to the fullest! I might put on a movie I like, read a book, or if the weather is nice I'll sit outside late at night and read or listen to an audiobook.

If I really don't care how late I go to bed, say, if it's a Friday or Saturday night, then I put the headphones on and bring on the Rush because I love few things more than good music but also know that listening to music gets me very worked up and that will delay my bedtime by at least one to two hours.

Having said all that, even if you're a tried-and-true night owl like me, if getting enough sleep is posing a real problem for you, this one is worth trying. Choose your desired bedtime based on how many hours of sleep you do best on, and if you use any sleep aids like melatonin, valerian, or others, set out the ones you take right at bedtime, and take others such as melatonin at their recommended times; in the case of melatonin that would be about two hours prior to bedtime.

Have any morning supplements or medications out and ready to go for the morning (such as, in my case, thyroid medication), and do what you need to do to make that plan work. You now have a nice, long list of tips and suggestions to get to sleep and stay asleep, so what do you have to lose?

What to Avoid in Order to Get Great Sleep

Here's where I'm going to become the bad guy, because there are a lot of very commonly used products, such as caffeine and alcohol, along with others like marijuana that are not nearly as prevalent but still commonly used, that will interfere with your ability to sleep well and on time, if not obliterate it. Certain prescriptions, along with over-the-counter drugs such as Sudafed (pseudoephedrine) and Bronkaid (ephedrine), can also wreak havoc on sleep, so avoid taking those if possible past noon, and avoid any 24-hour extended release version of these products. Certain antidepressants like Wellbutrin (bupropion), which work in part by increasing norepinephrine (also known as noradrenaline) levels in the brain, can also interfere with sleep if taken too late in the day.

First, my personal story on this topic: I used to be a moderate to heavy drinker, usually moderate on weeknights then all out on weekends. This "habit" started, ironically, because it was my way of falling asleep back in the days of having to get up extra early for a waste-of-time daily sales meeting.

When I decided to try giving up alcohol as an experiment in self-improvement, I was expecting to have the usual withdrawal symptoms I'd read about, but evidently I wasn't enough of a heavy drinker to get those. What I did get astonished me: *sleep*!

In fact, I slept 12–14 hours each night for about a month after ditching the wine and booze. This puzzled me at first, because insomnia is perhaps the most well-known and common alcohol withdrawal symptom. That's because alcohol works rather like Xanax and when you come off it, the brain's GABA receptors are no longer bound and your nervous system gets excessively excited. Hence why really hardcore alcoholics have to be hospitalized to avoid risk of seizures and death from delirium tremens.

What actually happened, or so my high-IQ mind has deduced, is that I'd long been depriving myself of high-quality, restful, deep sleep (or phase 4 sleep), and my body was suddenly making up for *a lot* of lost time.

You see, there's a popular myth that rapid eye movement, or REM sleep, is the restorative phase of sleep. However, that isn't true. This is the phase of sleep where dreams occur. It's only in deep, or phase 4 sleep that brain activity drops to producing slow, delta waves, and it is the deepest and most restorative phase of sleep. There is no dreaming in this phase. That's why people who are suddenly awakened while in phase 4 deep sleep will commonly be entirely disoriented and not even know where or possibly even who they are for a few minutes after.

And that's where alcohol was throwing me off and keeping me chronically fatigued: It interferes with phase 4 deep sleep.

After that experience I moved on to the next experiment and tried giving up caffeine. Knowing that doing so causes intensely brutal withdrawal headaches, I tapered off over four weeks by gradually mixing in decaf with my regular beans, then moving to decaf entirely for a little while (decaf still contains some caffeine), then green tea, then stopping altogether.

The result? *Wow!* Talk about an amazing, huge, incredible increase in energy levels! All those years coffee was beating up on my adrenals, just as it's doing to you if you drink the stuff. (Hey, I warned you that I might get preachy here about this stuff!)

With that, let's get into some specifics.

Alcohol

Alcohol, or more properly, ethanol, the kind found in alcoholic drinks, has long been used as a "nightcap" to help one get to sleep easier, and it will indeed do that—have you ever been passed out drunk or know someone who has? That isn't sleep; it's just being passed out drunk. This is largely where the misconception that alcohol can assist with getting a good night's rest comes from.

Alcohol, once in the bloodstream, rapidly binds to the brain's GABA receptors. Remember that GABA is the calming or relaxing neurotransmitter, the same one that the benzodiazepines bind to, as well as magnesium to a much smaller degree. It's the activation of GABA by alcohol that provides the relaxation and drowsiness it's known for.

However, there are two huge problems with this that prevent you from truly getting a solid night's sleep after drinking alcohol. The first I've already touched on: The fact that it interferes with stage 4, or deep sleep.

During deep sleep, the brain produces slow-wave sleep patterns called delta waves. This does occur with alcohol in the body; however, alcohol simultaneously causes alpha activity to occur. Alpha activity is not normal during sleep, but rather occurs with conscious relaxation and resting.

The other problem with alcohol is that you won't sleep through the night after an evening of drinking. First, as with drugs like Xanax, the GABA-binding activity wears off rather quickly, and the rebound effect wakes you up. The common misconception is that alcohol turns into sugar and the sugar rush wakes you up; however, alcohol is not converted into sugar, nor is it a sugar, nor can any alcohol be a sugar any more than a fat can be a carbohydrate.

What alcohol is actually converted to in the liver is acetaldehyde, the chemical responsible for hangovers. Again, sugar and what kind of alcohol you drank, in relation to how bad of a hangover to expect, is also total mythology. It is acetaldehyde, and only acetaldehyde, that causes the hangover effect, and of course the dehydrating effect of alcohol contributes to the morning headache and fatigue. Acetaldehyde is a very toxic substance and your liver works overtime to get rid of it.

Eventually, acetaldehyde is finally converted into water and carbon dioxide, at which time it is eliminated from the body.

The other reason alcohol can put you to sleep easily is that it increases the production of adenosine, which I'll also touch on in the caffeine discussion, which is a sleep- or drowsiness-inducing chemical in the brain. Just like with the GABA rebound effect, adenosine doesn't stick around through the night and also contributes to you finding yourself wide awake in bed four or so hours after crashing.

Other less technical, but equally problematic, effects of drinking alcohol include the fact that it's a diuretic and causes water to be eliminated from your body. That's why a night of drinking is followed by one or more nighttime bathroom trips, which ruin your sleep. It also causes breathing problems by causing muscles to become overly relaxed, hence why people who don't normally snore can keep the entire house awake after a night of drinking!

In summary, alcohol is the last thing you want to consume, except maybe for caffeine, before going to bed if you expect to sleep well and wake up feeling rested and rejuvenated.

Caffeine

This one is more obvious in terms of understanding why it disrupts sleep: Caffeine is a stimulant.

Before getting too technical, let's visit the biological half-life of caffeine. Half-life is defined as the time it takes for your body to get rid of half of the active drug in your body. So, for a simple example, say you drink a big mug of coffee on your way to work. Your body will take 5–6 hours to eliminate only 50% of your morning caffeine intake.

Using a half-life calculator, I did some math based on consuming 200 mg of caffeine in the morning, which is less than most coffee drinkers realize they consume, along with a 5.5-hour half-life. Based on that, I would have 50% or 100 mg in my body 6 hours later, 25% or 50 mg 11 hours later, and 13%, or 25 mg, 17 hours later.

Are you beginning to see the problem with caffeine?

At issue isn't that you only drank it in the morning and should be good to go by bedtime. The hard reality is that you still have active caffeine in your body at bedtime. Let's say you had that coffee at 8:00 a.m. and go to bed at 11:00 p.m. If you drank 200 mg of caffeine at eight, about the same amount in a large Starbucks drip coffee, you're going to have about 35 mg or so of active caffeine still in your body at bedtime.

Double those numbers for the amount most coffee drinkers actually consume, combined with the astonishing amount of foods, beverages, and even medications that contain caffeine.

Every fall, my kids' school has an event called Donuts with Dads. I take them to school and we hang out on the playground for thirty minutes enjoying coffee and donuts, and hot cocoa for the kids. It's at 7:30 a.m., which never amuses me, and I can't help but notice that while I'm holding my little Styrofoam cup of coffee, virtually all the other dads are walking around with huge plastic mugs in their hands!

In my research I learned that many people who use those big mugs and have two or more are actually consuming upwards of 900 mg or so every day! Based on caffeine's half-life, these guys are going to bed with somewhere around 150 mg of caffeine still active—more than two espresso shots! It's little wonder that so many people are chronically fatigued and just can't seem to catch up on sleep. It's because their morning "jolt" is still jolting them at midnight. What's worse is that caffeine's infamous "crash" keeps them drinking more and more throughout the day, compounding the negative effects.

Speaking of a caffeine crash, let's revisit adenosine, the fatigue-inducing neurotransmitter.

Caffeine keeps you awake (actually stressed) in two ways. First, it releases the stress hormones cortisol and epinephrine (adrenaline) in order to activate the fight-or-flight response. It's this caffeine-induced stress that masquerades as "energy." In reality, caffeine doesn't give you any energy at all. It merely puts you into the same situation as a caveman facing a lion. The same fight-or-flight response is activated, and if you've ever had an adrenaline dump, as I've experienced while doing advanced firearms combat training with law enforcement officers, you'll know that it massively increases alertness, situational awareness, and also has other effects such as shaking hands, sweaty palms, and tunnel vision.

While research at Johns Hopkins University has shown that caffeine does increase alertness and cognitive ability on the "up" swing and during the "high," it equally inhibits those same functions during the "down" phase, entirely negating any so-called benefits you believe you may be getting from it.

Speaking of the down phase and subsequent crash, that's where adenosine comes into play. The other way caffeine causes heightened wakefulness is by binding and occupying the brain's adenosine receptors, *preventing them from being activated.*

In response to caffeine, like any drug, the body builds a tolerance, causing the coffee drinker to gradually need more and more to get the same effect. That's because, in response to caffeine clogging up the adenosine receptors, the brain simply creates more and more of them.

The end result? The added adenosine receptors have a compound effect, and when the caffeine starts to lose effect—*boom!* Adenosine takes over and you experience the so-called "crash" of caffeine. What is really happening is that the sleepiness-inducing neurotransmitter has expanded its capacity in the brain in response to caffeine consumption and it fights like hell to bring you back "down."

Finally, caffeine has long-term implications on your endocrine system and HPA axis. The constant release of cortisol and epinephrine from your adrenal glands eventually wears them out over time. For a long time my office was near the best coffee shop I've ever experienced anywhere, Local Coffee in San Antonio, Texas.

For a few years I was having as many as six double espressos every day!

And then it happened: I found myself in the throes of what many might mistake as chronic fatigue syndrome, but in reality was adrenal exhaustion. Beating up my adrenal glands with daily, high caffeine intake gradually depleted their ability to keep up, and soon they weren't producing enough cortisol for normal daily functioning.

I was completely wiped out. There was no "pushing through"—it was like trying to drive a car, not on fumes, but rather with the gas tank missing entirely. It's impossible to do so, and it had negative effects on both my personal and professional lives.

My physician sent me to see a nutritionist, who set me up with certain adaptogens, which are herbs and supplements that help your body to adapt to circumstances. About six months later my cortisol levels were perfectly normal and I never went back to that crazy high caffeine consumption, although I'll still have a small cup if I feel like I need it in the morning, or just want to enjoy a good cup of coffee. (I've become a big fan of Black Rifle Coffee Company! Erring on the side of caution though, I get only their low-caffeine light roasts delivered.)

Finally, caffeine, like alcohol, has a strong dehydrating effect on the body. For each cup of coffee you drink, you need to consume two cups of water to replace what your liver needed to use to get rid of the caffeine. Just being able to avoid the endless bathroom visits while I'm trying to work during the day, all thanks to caffeine's diuretic effect, is enough to keep me away from becoming a regular caffeine consumer again!

Marijuana (Cannabis)

With marijuana legalization sweeping the country, I felt it necessary to include it here because the marijuana industry works hard to perpetuate the myth that it's a "medical" sleep aid. (According to them, marijuana is a cure-all for everything and we can just shut down the pharmaceutical industry. Yeah, right.) In reality, it's yet another substance that will wreck the restorative phases of your sleep just like alcohol does. Wait, let me correct myself— marijuana affects *all* five phases of sleep, some good, some bad.

Stage 1 sleep is the initial stage and lasts usually about 10 minutes. Cannabis actually helps with this by providing a relaxing sensation that assists with entering Stage 1 sleep, in part by increasing adenosine activity.

Stage 2 sleep is still light sleep, albeit for a longer duration, and here, cannabis has minimal negative impact.

Stage 3 and Stage 4 sleep, the more restful and restorative stages, particularly Stage 4, have a complex relationship with cannabis. Depending on what type of strain you're consuming, these stages can be interrupted or they can be prolonged.

The problem is with its most popularly known constituent, 9-delta-tetrahydrocannabinol, or THC, which tends to produce an activating or excitatory response during sleep; however, in very low doses, this does not occur.

The other most commonly known of the over 100 chemicals found in cannabis, cannabidiol or CBD, is known for countering the effects of THC. That's why so many medical marijuana strains are high in CBD; the idea is to get the benefits to the user without the "high" and its associated cognitive impairment.

Having said that, growers in the recreational marijuana industry, which is rapidly outgrowing the medical marijuana industry, have been working hard to completely breed CBD out of their products and get the THC level to insanely high amounts, guaranteeing that the user will get a very intense high, very quickly.

Even with consuming CBD only, research has produced conflicting results and it appears that the timing of administration and dosage of CBD is crucial as to whether it will help or hurt your sleep, and if you're consuming the plant/flower and not a pill produced by a pharm company, there's literally no way of knowing how many milligrams you have consumed, making such calculations impossible.

Finally, there's REM sleep, sometimes referred to as Stage 5. REM sleep is when dreaming occurs, which many research scientists believe is the brain's way of releasing old, useless, and random memories, freeing up space for new ones. Other aspects of dreaming are not understood, other than the fact that it's a necessary and required phase of sleep for maintaining good health as well as sanity.

Cannabis absolutely interferes with REM sleep, and this is where it fails as a sleep aid. Cannabis use decreases REM sleep and dreaming, primarily due to its blunting of dopamine. Dopamine, the "feel good" neurotransmitter, is what floods your brain when you're highly aroused and about to have sex with someone. It also floods your brain in response to drugs that produce a high, and as such it's also known as the "addiction" neurotransmitter since it's the dopamine response people get psychologically addicted to, and not the drug itself. (This of course is not the case with drugs that cause *physical* addiction, although psychological addiction frequently precedes it.)

The reason why recreational drug users have to take higher and higher doses over time to get the same effect is because the dopamine response becomes blunted. This is particularly true with drugs like cocaine, which so deplete dopamine that it's common for recovering addicts to become severely depressed. That is, in part, why antidepressants that increase dopamine levels have been developed. One of these is bupropion, commonly prescribed for smoking cessation.

Finally, frequency and duration of cannabis use also determine its effects on sleep quality. A study published in the *Journal of Addictive Diseases* found that daily cannabis users had significantly higher rates of insomnia when compared with occasional users. If you enjoy cannabis, or take it medically, a periodic tolerance break will help with this.

Morning Madness

While millions of people manage to get hooked on prescription sleep aids, there are a myriad of herbal and nutritional supplements that can do the job just as well without the addiction and side effects, albeit not instantly. In addition, most people seem unaware that commonly consumed substances can have extremely detrimental effects on the quality of your sleep. Finally, being a night owl forced to comply with society's morning-centric schedule doesn't have to be impossible; following the nighttime and morning suggestions found in this chapter are a great way to make life easier for owls.

Mitigating the Health Risks of Early Rising

Stay Healthy and Let the Early Birds "Sleep When They're Dead"

In this chapter I'm going to cover one thing, and one thing only, and how to reduce and modulate its effects: cortisol.

Cortisol, the body's stress hormone, is found to be chronically elevated in early risers as well as night owls forced to get up early. While cortisol is essential for normal functioning and you'd die a very fast death without it, having too much of it will absolutely, positively put you in an early grave. And our morning-obsessed society is killing people by forcing them to get up early and therefore keep their cortisol levels chronically elevated.

With that in mind, here are some easy and simple ways to lower your body's cortisol levels. (Note: You should check your levels first using a diurnal saliva cortisol test kit, which can be obtained from your doctor, or online, including Amazon, with all lab fees included. I consider the occasional test a bargain in exchange for knowing where my levels are and the ability to take corrective action when they're off.)

Eat Healthy

This probably sounds simplistic, but think about it: How often do you eat foods that are not particularly good for you?

By "healthy" I'm referring to "cortisol lowering." This includes avoiding a high-sugar diet or simple carbs in general, avoiding trans fats and refined fats, avoiding or limiting caffeine and alcohol (duh!), making sure your nutritional needs are met with quality vitamins and supplements, and eating enough healthy fats and protein.

Now, when most people think of a "healthy" fat, they think of something like olive oil, which is indeed good for you. However, with the cover blown off the lipid hypothesis, medical science has found that saturated fats are actually good for you. Yes, you heard me right: Saturated fats are healthy. I can't tell you how many times I've run something by my doctor and his response was, "Eat more fat!" (It's good to have a young doctor who is actually up to date on this stuff; it seems like most of my older relatives are taking statin drugs, known to cause dementia, because their doctors went to med school an eternity ago and don't keep current. Or maybe they're just beholden to their pharm rep. Who knows.)

Check out the book *Eat Fat, Get Thin: Why the Fat We East Is the Key to Sustained Weight Loss and Vibrant Health* by Mark Hyman, MD (Little, Brown and Company, 2016). As you may have deduced, it was my own doctor who recommended the book, and I can indeed state that once I put it into practice, I lost fat, put on muscle, and just generally feel better eating a diet rich in saturated fats. The author also has an accompanying cookbook in print to make the journey easier.

Relax, Relax, Relax!

When I'm stressed, my wife tells me to go shooting. Spending an hour or so at a shooting range with some of my favorite guns is extremely therapeutic for me and I walk out happy, upbeat, and relaxed. However, you don't have to be a gun slut like me to achieve relaxation. There are many ways to do that, some of which you already know work for you, so here are some of the more effective ones I've found.

Meditation

For a long time I struggled with the idea of meditation, and wrote it off as new-age bullshit. However, I went back to it, persisted, tried out a different meditation app on my iPhone (also recommended by my doctor), and found myself taking to it like a fish to water. What made the change for me was learning that everyone fails at meditation. Everyone. In mindfulness practice, only an enlightened person can literally clear his or her mind and eliminate all thoughts, and the only known enlightened person in history was the Buddha himself. Even Buddhist monks who have practiced 20 years or more openly admit they always "fail" at meditation.

Fail or no fail—well, fail—I can tell you that it works. And I don't mean grabbing the phone and earbuds when I'm stressed or can't sleep or whatever. I'm talking about how meditating 10 minutes a day, which I split into two five-minute sessions, has a dramatic and positive effect on my relaxation and even my overall happiness.

The app I use is called Simple Habit, and there are now many apps available, including the industry leader, Headspace. Try one or more by using the free versions and find which one works best for you, then set a daily reminder to meditate for five minutes a day to start. You'll be amazed at the changes in yourself, especially after you understand and accept that just about everyone "fails" at it. With that internal pressure to keep all thoughts out of my head gone, meditation suddenly changed from a challenge into a gift for me.

Deep Breathing

There are many deep-breathing exercises, far too many to count; however, a steady practice of deep breathing will have amazing therapeutic effects on your stress and therefore cortisol levels, regardless of which you choose.

Perhaps the most well-known deep-breathing exercise is the "4 × 4" method, taught to U.S. military troops to use in the heat of battle to reduce stress. It consists of inhaling deeply for four seconds, holding it for four seconds, breathing out and emptying your lungs for four seconds, then another four-second hold before breathing in again.

What I found to be very effective is the Yogic 4–7–8 technique popularized by Dr. Andrew Weil, who learned it while visiting India. It consists of taking a rapid, deep breath in through your nose for four seconds, holding it for seven, breathing out forcefully through your mouth to make a "whoosh" sound for eight seconds, and then repeating the process. He and his associate at the University of Arizona Medical School, Dr. Steven Gurgevich, have both reported seeing dramatic improvements in anxiety patients through the use of this technique.

At home, when one of the kids gets all upset and worked up, my wife or I will ask them to take some deep breaths, and if necessary, we'll do it with them so they can follow along.

Trust me, it works. If you're the parent of young children, you'll thank me after you try it!

Self-hypnosis

This should fall under the "Relax" category but I broke it out separately because of the incredible, positive effects it had in alleviating my stress and anxiety during a grueling 18-month IRS audit covering two years of both business and personal tax returns.

That's also how I know of Dr. Steven Gurgevich—I used his "Relieve Anxiety with Medical Hypnosis" on a daily basis to achieve that outcome. He has many others, such as RelaxRx and dozens more on his website, with many available at Audible.

Unlike meditation, which, while guided with an app, is still something you actually do on your own, with medical hypnotherapy you mostly just relax and listen. You'll be asked to do some breathing exercises to become deeply relaxed, as well as some guided imagery. All I know is that it works. For me, anyway.

I say "for me" because medical hypnosis is only effective if you believe it will be. If you're a naysayer, or believe that all hypnosis is the equivalent of a Las Vegas hypnotist comedy show, you'll block your mind from going into trance, either consciously or unconsciously. Either way, I recommend giving it a try. For me it's my first-line treatment when I'm especially stressed or anxious.

Exercise—Within Reason

If you're like most people who go to a gym to work out, you can't help but notice the regulars who carry around gallon jugs of water and intently watch themselves doing bicep curls in the mirror.

When I say exercise within reason, what I'm saying is that you don't have to become one of these self-absorbed muscle-head types. In fact, that's one of the worst things you can do for your stress levels! My gym expressly prohibits gallon jugs of water, loud grunting, and tank tops. Be dignified or GTFO is their modus operandi.

Heavy lifting like that increases cortisol levels. This is why professional bodybuilders and their trainers learn so much about how to delicately balance lifting hard with maintaining healthy cortisol levels, since cortisol is muscle-destroying, or catabolic. What most men, and some women, do in the gym is to lift and lift until they can't lift anymore. However, past a certain point, the benefits disappear and cortisol takes over. It not only negates the benefits that more moderate lifting would have provided, it also wrecks your health in general, as you already know.

I learned the pitfalls of typical weight training from a friend who is himself a bodybuilder. (And no, he's not like those regulars at all.) He limits his workouts to a surprisingly short amount of time each day—as in under 10 minutes—and the man is *huge*. He wasn't always that way, either; we were also friends about 10 years ago when he let himself go, lost muscle, and put on a belly. He got back to all his bodybuilding hugeness with those surprisingly short workouts!

So, whether you do cardio, weights, Pilates, barre, or anything else, do it in moderation. Excessive exercise raises cortisol levels, which in turn raise your stress level and damage your health.

Use Adaptogens

Remember when I said my low cortisol, and subsequently high cortisol, was cured through the use of adaptogens? There are several that have particular benefit for your adrenal glands and your cortisol levels in turn.

Those that I have used are ashwaganda (probably the best of the bunch in my experience), astragalus, licorice root (be aware that this can be stimulating—avoid at night), holy basil, and rhodiola. And of course magnesium glycinate, which does wonders for stress whenever it rears its ugly head.

Again, I'm not a doctor, nor do I play one on television, so please, consult with your own healthcare provider prior to heading over to Amazon and ordering any of these!

Spend Enough Time Outdoors

We humans weren't evolved to live inside man-made houses with artificial lighting.

Humans have spent nearly all of their time on earth living outdoors. When you consider that evolution lags by about 100,000 years, it's easy to see why artificial lights and blue screens trash our sleep so badly. We simply haven't evolved and adapted to them yet.

Getting outdoors doesn't mean you have to spend a weekend camping in the woods. It can be a 20-minute walk on your lunch break. It can be getting outside the moment you get out of bed, which has the added benefit of helping your body to adapt to waking at that time. It can be a daily morning walk on the beach, which my wife and I did almost every day while living in Southern California prior to escaping to Texas.

Use Essential Oils

I'm not the expert in this department—my wife is. She has a nice collection of essential oils she uses for herself as well as for our girls. If one is having trouble sleeping, or has a night terror, she'll grab just the right oil and the problem is magically solved.

I don't think this is a placebo effect, either. One day at the drugstore I grabbed a vial of lavender essential oil for myself, and boy, does it truly promote relaxation.

I've gotten into the habit of putting a couple of drops on my pillow (remember, this stuff is concentrated) and a little dab on my upper chest. I really do get relaxed and sleep much more quickly than without it.

Like I said, I'm not an expert on essential oils and there are a myriad of books, websites, and articles dedicated to them. However, lavender is best known as the relaxing essential oil, so I'd start there.

Sleep!

This one is BIG, because insufficient sleep has a direct and very dramatic effect on cortisol levels. The bottom line is if you don't get enough sleep, you're going to have chronically elevated cortisol levels, will be at risk for a very long list of serious diseases, and will literally shorten your life, and I mean in terms of a decade or more, not just a few months.

Also, since this chapter is about how to mitigate the risks of early rising if you're forced to do so, it's worth mentioning again that virtually all naturally early risers, who are not forced to get up early but just wake up at that time, also have chronically elevated cortisol levels and shorter life expectancies.

I'm not going to go into specifics on how to get a good night's sleep since that was covered in the previous chapter. What I want to emphasize is getting enough sleep.

For a night owl like me, the trick isn't getting up, it's getting to sleep on time. And I misused alcohol for years to achieve this, not realizing that I wasn't actually getting enough sleep although I thought I did. That would certainly explain my ongoing fatigue and the need for large amounts of coffee throughout the day. And that's another reason I advocate neither alcohol nor caffeine consumption; it creates a vicious downward spiral of stimulant-then-depressant, over and over, every day, ad infinitum, ad nauseam, ad mortem.

Go back and review the previous chapter. Once you can consistently get to sleep on time every night, you'll find that you're getting enough sleep—finally—and your cortisol and therefore stress levels will drop. You'll also find yourself in better health overall and feeling better.

A Word of Caution

Even though I've described the highly addictive nature of so-called tranquilizers and sleeping pills, along with alcohol, the reality is that we live in a "quick-fix" society. Antidepressants didn't come along due to medical necessity; they came along because psychiatrists have largely changed their practice from weekly sessions of talk therapy to a monthly five-minute visit to get a prescription refill. Antidepressants are also extremely physically addictive, with a few exceptions like Wellbutrin.

My point is that you must avoid the temptation to look for the quick fix. I don't doubt for one second that the majority of readers who saw the word "relax" had their minds immediately go to thoughts of a pill to make that happen. That's the world we live in, and the strong desire for instant gratification has sadly extended to medicine. Instead of recommending medical hypnotherapy, or meditation, or deep breathing, or any proven relaxation technique, far too many doctors will whip out the prescription pad and hook you up with Xanax or another tranquilizer, and before you know it you're hooked and can't stop without running the risk of very dangerous withdrawal symptoms like seizures.

A final thought on stress: I'm not saying you have to eliminate it. No one can do that. You just have to work on managing and reducing it. It's well known that being President of the United States is likely the single most stressful job in the world. That's why presidents age so very rapidly while in office, and why health fanatics like George W. Bush end up with 95% clogged arteries thanks to chronically high cortisol.

It's also why most presidents in recent history work out. That includes George W. Bush, as mentioned, his dad, George H.W. Bush, Bill Clinton, and Barack Obama. I'm not so sure about President Trump, given his physique, but then again, he's been living on the edge all of his life and being the president is probably just like any typical day at the Trump Tower office was for him in terms of stress.

Even when I met Congressman Paul Ryan, and asked how members from both parties are such good friends despite attacking each other on the floor during debate, he said half the reason is that they're all in the Capitol gym every morning working out together! See, those guys know how to manage stress, too!

Morning Madness

In a truly just world, we'd be able to sue employers for the damaged health and shortened life expectancies their morning schedules cause us through elevated cortisol. While seemingly simplistic, the methods explained in this chapter do work for reducing both stress and cortisol. As always, check with your doctor before jumping head first into a new routine.

15

How Flexible Work Hours Benefit Employers

Why Employers Who Force Morning Schedules Are Losing Money

The solution to the dilemma of the night owl, and the employer seeking top talent, is flexible work hours.

This has become popular overseas, particularly in Europe as well as in South America; however, the United States hasn't caught on yet. We're still stuck on the machismo, "early bird gets the worm" mythology. And yet, these very same employers who demand their employees show up first thing the morning are actually shooting themselves in the foot and are losing money.

Flexible Work Schedules Benefit Employers

First of all, flexible work schedules aren't a pass for "laziness" or "slothfulness," as American society would have us believe. Rather, they're a way for employers to attract top talent—for example, I sure as hell wouldn't accept a job offer that required me to be there no later than eight o'clock, and this would be the employer's loss. In addition, flexible work schedules accommodate the natural sleep schedules of night owls, as well as avoiding harm to their health. With the legal industry always looking for new causes for lawsuits, and the evidence now piled up miles high that early rising really does harm to a night owl's health and puts him or her at risk for premature death, it's only a matter of time before lawyers get on the bandwagon and fight for our best interests. And I think that's going to happen sooner rather than later.

The following sections offer some ways that flex work schedules benefit employers.

Heightened Employee Morale

As mentioned throughout the book, a happy worker is a productive worker. Why, then, would an employer deliberately and intentionally make a good employee *unhappy*, thus harming their productivity?

The biggest reason for providing the option of a flexible work schedule to employees is the simple fact that they're going to be happier, more awake and alert, more productive, and, most important, will feel a sense of satisfaction and a distinct fondness for that employer. An employer can reduce turnover, which benefits the business.

I can tell you right now that, despite having unlocked the secrets to the sales profession, if I didn't like my boss, I didn't perform. Plain and simple.

Remember the best sales manager I've ever had, the one who explained that cold calling is a waste of time? He also didn't require anyone to come in early. In fact, he didn't care if we came in, or even worked at all, as long as we produced our numbers each month.

This is how businesses operate in the real world. When a business hires an outside contractor, or a management consultant, there is neither any requirement nor any expectation for that contractor or consultant to show up at eight every day. No, what matters is that the job gets done. And my old manager understood this. That's why he had the top office in the entire West, and why he was able to retire very comfortably far in advance of his peers.

After he retired, a new manager came in with her ideas of "being on time." The two other top reps in the office and I said, "Screw this shit," lined up new jobs, and quit. In fact there's been tons of speculation about what exactly caused the demise of Lucent Technologies. This was a large part of it, a shift away from performance-based work to hourly-based work and an expectation to be in the office even when there was no reason at all to be there.

Any employer who wants to attract the very best, top talent *must* begin offering flexible work hours! How do you think Silicon Valley manages to constantly stay on the cutting edge? Simple: It's because it's the only place in the United States where flexible work schedules are the norm. That's right, *they're the norm*, not the exception. There is no sleep-shaming in Silicon Valley and that's why tech companies in other areas, those who utilize a strict, 8-to-5 work schedule simply can't keep up, and meanwhile they scratch their heads wondering why.

Increased Sense of Fairness and Job Satisfaction

At the London School of Economics and Political Science, researchers Leslie Henry and T. Alexandra Beauregard found that a key element for an employee to achieve a proper work-life balance is that they're being treated fairly and given the ability to make the most of their opportunity with their employer.

Why is this important? That one is easy: It's because of the law of reciprocity. When an employee feels that they're not being given the most favorable circumstances to prosper and achieve, they foster a strong sense of resentment against their employers, much like myself and the other top reps at my old job felt, causing us to, first, interview for other jobs on that employer's time, and subsequently to quit without notice. (In that industry, even with a two-week notice, you got five minutes to get your stuff and get out, complete with a security escort. However, by law the employer still had to pay those two weeks' salary, so they got screwed both ways—all because they demanded we be in every day at 8:00 a.m.!)

When an employer is providing favorable circumstances to prosper and succeed, just as my "best sales manager ever" did, employees feel a strong sense of appreciation, and, more important, *obligation* to perform at their very best for that employer.

In plain English, flex hours are a win-win for employers because they enjoy higher productivity and output from that employee, just as I set new sales records out of a sense of obligation to a boss who was giving me what I needed to succeed—flex hours.

Better and More Qualified Employees

While tons of employers will turn up their nose at this and self-righteously proclaim that a good employee is one who is in the office at seven, the truth is that the economy is flying high right now and prospective employees have choices. Here in the Dallas–Fort Worth Metroplex, as I write this, there is a shortage of available employees and about 500,000 good jobs that are unfilled as a result.

Here's a wake-up call: If you're an employer who requires a morning-based work schedule, you're simply not going to get the talent you require in this strong economy. *Top-talent night owls have other choices,* better *choices.* They're not going to just sit back and let you walk all over them with your "early bird gets the worm" bullshit.

Millennials in particular are strongly averse to morning-centric schedules, and they now make up about 35% of the American workforce—that's over one-third! And contrary to popular belief, the millennials I know happen to have a strong sense that hard work and smart work equates to success, and many are very entrepreneurial. With the Internet at their fingertips, why would they work for you and drag themselves to work at 8:00 a.m. or earlier when they can start an Internet business, or find an employer who "gets it"?

If you want to attract top talent among millennials, you have no other choice but to offer flex hours. Sorry, but that's the hard truth. I'm not here to give you a shoulder to cry on, I'm here to give you the truth. And as the old movie quote goes, if you're still resisting this and demanding that everyone come in by eight, *you can't handle the truth!*

On the other hand, if you make it clear that you can offer flexible hours in your job postings, you're massively increasing the pool of available, top-qualified talent who will be willing to work for you.

Reduced Turnover

Turnover is a four-letter word for business owners and employers. It's unbelievably costly, and in fact, one of the reasons my Never Cold Call Again® sales training programs have finally come to be embraced by employers is because dropping the requirement to cold call has a huge, positive effect on salesperson turnover, specifically because it's well-proven and documented that a requirement to make cold calls is the number one cause of sales force turnover.

The happier, more satisfied, and more obligated an employee feels toward you, the chances of that employee leaving for greener grass drops dramatically. In other words, let them work when they're feeling their best, and you won't have to endure endless turnover like most employers do.

Studies have even shown that, particularly among younger workers, money isn't the top factor they consider when choosing whom to work for, or whether to jump ship to a better job. No, flexibility is one of the top factors that's most important to them, and by denying flexibility, you're denying yourself access to top talent.

Fewer Sick Days or PTO Days

I can tell you from personal experience that I missed many days of work, at least at those jobs that demanded I be in the office by eight. That obviously caused the employer lost productivity, and cost me PTO days. Offering flexible work hours reduces absenteeism, plain and simple.

When I had flexible hours, I produced way above and beyond my sales quotas, regardless of whether I worked on any particular day or not. Smart employers look only at the numbers, not at the number of missed days and/or tardiness. In fact, "tardiness" is an obsolete word that applies only to school kids now.

In summary, by opting to offer flex hours, employers will have happier employees, healthier employees, more productive employees, more loyal and dedicated employees, less resentment, reduced turnover, and so many more benefits that there are too many to list here.

Morning Madness

Employers who are stuck on the macho "earlier is better" nonsense are actually hurting themselves in terms of lost productivity and revenue, and overall business success. The key to prospering in the twenty-first century is to offer flexible work schedules to employees. If you want to attract top talent, you must make it clear and apparent in job listings that flex hours are an option; otherwise top talent that isn't interested in getting up before down simply won't apply.

Epilogue

Night Owls Have a Huge Advantage over Early Risers

If you have suffered a lifetime of sleep-shaming, have been made to feel lazy or inferior or useless because you don't jump out of bed before dawn, if you have lost good jobs or been unable to accept new ones because you're a night owl, fret no more.

Night owls:

Are smarter than early risers
Are more creative than early risers
Are more resilient than early risers
Enjoy dramatically more productive hours each day than early risers
Are more productive than early risers
Don't "crash" by mid-afternoon and can keep going and going.
Are more relaxed people, overall

And, of course, they have many other advantages over early risers that have been discussed in this book.

You've also seen the dark side of life as a night owl: the brainwashing society seems to subject everyone to, and the subsequent feeling of imprisonment by ostracized night owls. You've learned how early rising is significantly harmful to your health, puts you at risk for myriad severe illnesses, and will shorten your life expectancy if it's not natural for you (and even if it is!)

You also know how to mitigate these health risks, how to make the most of a bad situation if you must rise early (though I hope you'll find another job rather than continue to tolerate that), and you have endless facts at your fingertips to convince skeptics and sworn early risers as to why it's not in their best interests to force you to continue to rise early.

In the end, night owls have a strong advantage over early risers.

We're the creators of the world. The people who make things happen. The writers. The inventors. The agents of change. The smartest. *The best.*

I sincerely thank you for reading this book. If you're a night owl, I hope you have the arsenal you need to both convince others of the truth, as well as to live better in a morning-centric society. If you're an early riser, you now know the harm, particularly in regard to health, that forced early rising causes to night owls. I hope you will consider the interests of night owls rather than just yours alone.

Happy late nights to you!

—Frank J. Rumbauskas

Acknowledgments

This book was far more time-consuming and difficult to write than any of my previous four books, for the simple reason that it required tremendous research in order to back up the claims made within.

First off and as always, I'd like to thank my wife, Dana, and my two girls, Agnes and Maeve, for all the time I spent in my office working on this book, including on weekends. They will be the first to tell you that I've been coming home brain-fried for months and wanting nothing other than simple relaxation after many, many days of researching and writing.

On that same note, sitting in an office chair for greatly extended hours, even a great one like the one I'm in now, can make one's back tight. For relief of back pain—permanent relief—I thank the late and great Dr. John Sarno, MD, for his groundbreaking work on the real causes and real solutions to back pain. If you suffer from back pain, to any degree, please check out his book *Healing Back Pain: The Mind-Body Connection* (Grand Central Publishing, 2001). I also thank my chiropractor and massage therapist, though I understand that their treatments have no impact on back pain but rather just feel good!

Special thanks goes out to Matt Holt and Shannon Vargo at John Wiley & Sons. I've only written business books in the past, and trying to sell a publisher on a book that covers brand-new territory, and away from what have been proven sellers for me, is no easy task. However, Matt and the editing team were very receptive, and once I was able to articulate the specific purpose of this book, they jumped on the opportunity to publish it. Thank you!

My physician, Dr. Anthony Lyssy, gets special thanks for giving me my life back after dealing with low thyroid and subsequently adrenal exhaustion. I also thank him for convincing me to give meditation another try after I'd given up on it, which has made a tremendous, positive improvement in my life. Thanks also to my ankle surgeon, Dr. Joseph Carr Vineyard, for installing that new ankle in early 2017 and *literally* giving me my life back!

Finally, my family, especially my parents, must get a lot of credit. Despite having to force me out of bed for years, they finally "get it" now. As much as I complain now about all the pressure to do well in school that I endured, my mom instilled a strong work ethic through that. And looking over my dad's shoulder as a kid as he read *Entrepreneur* magazine allowed me to see the forest through the trees and come to realize that there are better and easier ways to make a great living than just a job. Thankfully the Internet Age has since spread that truth far and wide.

Last but not least, ironic as this may sound, I thank every boss I've had in years past who made me get up before dawn to be in the office by 7:30 or 8:00 a.m. You motivated me to create this book and save many others from the same hell!

About the Author

The late Frank Rumbauskas had a lot of labels: *New York Times* best-selling author, sales guru, top Internet marketer, success mentor, Google-Certified AdWords Expert, and many more.

Frank's rise to success began in the in-your-face world of outside sales, where he learned the hard way that chasing prospects and goals only kept them out of reach. While working as an account executive for a Fortune 100 company, Frank did what he was told and chased every prospect. He cold called, he went through the traditional steps of a sale that he was taught, he placed prospects and customers first, and as a result he experienced nothing but failure and frustration.

Then, Frank learned about the science of social dynamics from a star performer and everything changed. This top producer took Frank under his wing, and explained the basics of why people buy, why one person has the power and the next doesn't, and how and why these principles apply in any and all situations, business or otherwise. Frank's sales results more than tripled—almost immediately—as a result of applying these principles.

Frank took these principles, perfected them, built systems around them, and applied them anywhere to get anything.

Frank left the sales profession at the top of his game, and helped others approach their work and lives from a position of power. A serial entrepreneur in industries including Internet, telecom, and insurance, Frank experienced explosive growth first-hand without using obsolete tactics that drain profits.

In addition to Frank's best-selling sales and marketing books, he was routinely featured as a top Internet marketing expert in seminars, webinars, and more. The reason was simple: while Frank was known as a best-selling author and top entrepreneur, it was his expertise in Internet marketing that got him there. Internet marketing was Frank's top passion, and the engine behind his financial freedom.

Frank was frequently quoted in mainstream media including *Entrepreneur*, *Investor's Business Daily*, and *Selling Power*, and his books continue to help sales leaders achieve their full potential.

Index